PRAISE

"I love this book—Dominica DeGrandis talks about the chronic problems
we all have in knowledge work and technology work in a way that is breezy,
familiar, and often irreverent, but also shows off decades of learnings
and concrete techniques we can quickly adopt, both at work and at home.
Also wonderfully rewarding is when DeGrandis describes the theory of
why these practices work, in a way that is accessible and enlightening."

GENE KIM, researcher, founder of IT Revolution, and coauthor
of *The DevOps Handbook* and *The Phoenix Project*

"The most practical book I've seen on making processes lean. Dominica's
deep experience coaching companies is fully on display as she walks the reader
through a series of exercises to find waste and eliminate it—or, in her
terms, to catch those sneaky 'time thieves' in the act. Read this on a Sunday
and you'll want to start trying out the exercises on Monday!"

MARK SCHWARTZ, former CIO of US Citizenship and Immigration Services
and author of *The Art of Business Value* and *A Seat at the Table*

"It is about time someone addresses time theft (aka the perfect crime)
head on. Not only does Dominica provide a lot of the why behind the forces
that cause us to make bad decisions about our time, she also provides
ideas of what to do about them. I wish I had this book when I took my first
management job!"

JULIA WESTER, Lean Consultant and Blogger at EverydayKanban.com

"Many of us wear our busyness as a badge of honor. In Making Work Visible,
Dominica DeGrandis shows us how we can make hidden work-in-process visible,
to clearly see the effect it has on our ability to get things done. Once we can see it,
she dives deep into the hidden aspects of our WIP that steal our time, energy,
and productivity, along with strategies for combating each of them. Making
Work Visible helps us to take a step back from all that busyness and really see."

CHRIS HEFLEY, Chief Revenue Officer, Retrium

Making Work Visible

EXPOSING TIME THEFT TO OPTIMIZE WORK & FLOW

DOMINICA DeGRANDIS
FOREWORD BY TONIANNE DeMARIA

IT REVOLUTION PRESS
PORTLAND, OR

25 NW 23rd Pl, Suite 6314
Portland, OR 97210

First Edition
Printed in the United States of America
10 9 8 7 6 5 4 3 2

Cover and interior book design by Belinda Bowling, Joy Stauber,
and Richard Weaver, Stauber Brand Studio
Cover and interior illustrations by Dominica DeGrandis
Author photograph by Laurence G. Cohen

Library of Congress Control Number: 2017948984

ISBN: 978-1942788157
ePub ISBN: 978-1942788164
Kindle ISBN: 978-1942788188
Web PDF ISBN: 978-1942788171

For information about special discounts for bulk purchases or for
information on booking authors for an event, please visit our website
at www.ITRevolution.com.

MAKING WORK VISIBLE

I dedicate this book to my greatest inspirers: my four brilliant children, Rachel, Robert, Angelo, and Augustus. You teach me more about life and joy than any career accomplishment possibly could.

CONTENTS

METRICS, FEEDBACK, AND CIRCUMSTANCES

LIST OF FIGURES

PART 3: METRICS, FEEDBACK, AND CIRCUMSTANCES

CONCLUSION: CALIBRATION

FOREWORD

Day, n. A period of twenty-four hours, mostly misspent.
—Ambrose Bierce

So about that internet meme, the one assuring our frazzled selves that *everyone* has the same twenty-four hours in their day as <insert entrepreneurial rock star here>.

I'd like to nip that bit of condescension in the bud and offer an emphatic, *Not quite*. While many of our business role models are in fact driven by a seemingly superhuman work ethic supported by 100+ hour work weeks, they nevertheless have an advantage over us mere mortals. While the number of minutes available to us each day might be the same, control over what we do with those hours differs significantly. When Elon Musk is faced with too much work-in-progress (WIP), he has the authority to delegate, deprioritize, or simply say *no*. When variation rears its head and a well-thought-out strategic plan no longer aligns with the organization's needs, Sheryl Sandberg has the ability to switch gears. And when Jeff Bezos is confronted with conflicting priorities, it is likewise doubtful he needs to seek direction via a convoluted bureaucracy to gain clarity over which course to follow.

When these things happen to us (and let's face it, they often do), we're faced with a very different set of repercussions than those of our billionaire counterparts.

So what about us? In the absence of unbridled agency and an extensive support staff, how do we do all that needs to get done, when it needs to get done, without sacrificing quality or our sanity in the process? In a culture that exalts productivity and perpetuates the mythology of multitasking, how do we maximize our time and our workflow to the point that our effort and our energy yields the greatest impact? Most importantly, how do we do all of that and still have time for living?

Time saved. Time spent. Time wasted. We frame conversations about time much in the way we do money. Ostensibly "free" but nevertheless invaluable, time is arguably one of the most precious resources we have, yet one we never seem to have enough of as individuals, as teams, or as organizations.

Anyone who has ever been faced with a deadline can certainly relate to Parkinson's Law: *work expands to fill the time available for its completion.* Let's be honest—when was the last time you completed quality work days or even hours ahead of deadline?

You're not alone.

It seems we're constantly *doing,* but doing what exactly? Why are our weeks filled with days where we return home exhausted, only to lament how we've barely made a dent in our to-dos? Like the elusive sock that mysteriously goes missing in the laundry, where do those lost hours go? Who—or rather *what*—is responsible for stealing our time, our focus, our energy?

The attempt to harness or "keep time" is in no way a modern or even premodern convention. Prehistoric humans tracked the phases of the moon. The Sumerians created the sexagesimal numeral system still in use today, employing sixty to divide the hour into minutes and then minutes into seconds. The Egyptians used obelisks to calculate the length of shadows cast by the sun. The shortcomings of solar-based measures became apparent the moment clouds appeared or the night sky arrived and so with clepsydras—or water clocks—the Persians and Greeks offered an alternative, monitoring water flow instead to measure the passage of time.

With these ancient time-tracking tools came the earliest forms of scheduling—when to plant crops and bring in the harvest, when to conduct commerce, and when to perform daily rituals such as eating or sleeping.

Fast forward to today. Despite all our modern "conveniences," effective time management has for many become an uphill battle, an all-consuming if not quixotic goal. While the Information Economy ushered in 24/7 connectivity, it likewise begot round-the-clock expectations, and so, paradoxically, technology like mobile phones and email and video conferencing—tools that would ostensibly make life easier—often enslave us. We allow the chaos of modern work coupled with an often paralyzing number of options at our disposal to overload us, to distract us, to stealthily steal our time and focus and ultimately impede our effectiveness.

We tend to fetishize the complex, but just as the earliest solutions for tracking time were both easily implemented and yielded extraordinary results, so too are the ideas detailed in *Making Work Visible: Exposing Time Theft to Optimize Work & Flow*. Much in the way sky, sun, sticks, and sand provided ancient man actionable, visual feedback, so too do the suggestions Dominica outlines in the pages that follow.

It should come as no surprise that we can better manage what we can see. When we can't see our work, our options are obscured. We're blind to our own capacity and we certainly can't communicate that capacity to others. The resultant mental overload creates stress. Stress compounds the work we already have, essentially contributing to WIP, compromising the ability to focus, prioritize, make decisions, and complete work with quality, let alone complete work at all.

The visualization and WIP-limiting strategies Dominica offers demystify our cognitive load; normalize expectations among team members; promote focus; situate work in its context, surfacing problems (and allowing for solutions to be made) in real time; and provide a clear path to completion with quality. Elegantly explained and deeply-insightful, the utility of the suggestions contained within cannot be overstated.

To be sure, it is no small irony in that I'm writing about "time theft" while spending a week aboard a sailboat exploring an archipelago in the Salish Sea beholden only to "island time." It's the first holiday where I've intentionally left my watch at home, instead choosing to be fully present to the wildlife and seascapes around me: bald eagles and peregrine falcons soar high above craggy bluffs where the pristine coastline meets old-growth forests. Otters gracefully propel themselves through the glassy surf, disrupting kelp and eelgrass in search of their next meal. Along the rockier parts of the shore, scores of sea lions loll in the sun, as hauled-out harbor seals nurse their spotted pups on a secluded beach nearby. A congregation of boats idling in the distance serves as a familiar sign, and it's not long before I too glimpse a family of orcas perform for their Nikon-wielding audience (affectionately known by locals as the "pod-parazzi") on crystalline jade waters that seemingly end at a cerulean blue sky.

If there was ever a place where I've given less thought to watching the clock, it is in this Pacific Northwest jewelbox known as the San Juan Islands.

This is precisely why Dominica's book is so important. Our culture of overwork, our obsession with productivity versus effectiveness, our default mode of existing rather than living—these things aren't simply unnatural and unhealthy, they're unsustainable—for the individual, for the team, for the organization's bottom line.

The thoughtful observations and easily implementable suggestions Dominica offers are the first step in helping create habits that lead to a virtuous cycle of healthy, sustainable, and improvable work. Work in which we experience more clarity, less stress, increased focus, improved decision-making, manageable workloads, and, by extension, a more fulfilling work day, which in turn affords us the slack needed to fully live our lives rather than simply chase productivity.

So while technically we have the same number of hours in a day as <insert entrepreneurial rockstar here>, it's creating thoughtful work systems that make us cognizant of what we use those hours for during the workday. And it is what those hours afford us the opportunity to do when we leave the office that makes for a fully integrated life.

Indeed, time is sacred. Treat it as such. Visualize your work. Limit the amount of work you take on. Pay attention to its flow. Build thoughtful work systems to reflect what really matters.

To breathe. To think. To learn. To grow. To play. To love. To live.

For it is in working well that we can live well. I am confident the wisdom Dominica offers in the pages that follow is the first step to achieving such existence so that you too can begin to experience less stolen time and instead plan for more island time.

Tonianne DeMaria
Orcas Island, Washington

INTRODUCTION: WORK AND FLOW

Do not squander time for that is the stuff life is made of.
—Benjamin Franklin

As a build engineer, my first job out of college was to make builds visible. This meant tracking which version of what file went on which computer and in what environment. Three months into that job, I was working on a *build*—getting all the code from the source code repository, compiling it into executables, and then installing the resulting new functionality into a place where others (analysts, developers, testers, and other interested people) could see it. The build wasn't compiling though, and I sat there troubleshooting the broken build, in the office, alone, at 2:00 a.m. Tired, I was making mistakes, so I went home. I seriously questioned my career choice. Technology work apparently meant working many late nights. After a nap, I returned to the office to track down code dependencies between various developers and eventually got the build working.

I'm not sure exactly how many hours I've spent tracking down dependencies during all my years of merging, building, and releasing software, but I'm convinced that it's been way too many. If I had a dollar for every minute spent troubleshooting builds and broken environments, I would have a sweet little nest egg. Delayed work, whether it is measured in hours, days, weeks, or even months, carries with it a cost. Losing time due to avoidable problems is expensive and dispiriting. Life is short. Wasted time can never be regained.

In the sci-fi film *In Time*, time is literally money—people earn minutes, hours, and days to buy food, housing, transportation, and everything else imaginable. Street thugs kill people by stealing all their minutes. Wasted time is the kiss of death. In one memorable scene, Will Salas, played by Justin Timberlake, saves the life of the wealthy Henry Hamilton, played by Matt Bomer. When Will and Henry get to a safe place, Henry tells Will that he is 105 years old  and tired of living. He asks twenty-eight-year-old Will what he would do with 100 years. Will quips back, "I sure as hell wouldn't waste it." Later, as Will sleeps, Henry gives Will his 100 years and leaves him a note, "Don't waste my time," before he runs off to time-out by allowing his own clock to run down while sitting on the ledge of a tall bridge.[1]

A scrawled note from a dystopian sci-fi film embodies our reality. Time is life—use time wisely.

We workers are drowning in nonstop requests for our time. From developers to IT operations people, it's overwhelming to keep up with the ever increasing demand. In this regard, things haven't changed much since my first job out of college, where as a software configuration management lead at Boeing, I did builds and deployments on IBM mainframes at Hickam Air Force Base in Hawaii.

A line of people formed outside my cube wanting to know the status of a build. Did everything compile okay? When will the build be deployed to the quality assurance environment? Can I get one last change in? I wanted to say, "Pick a number. I'm working as fast as I can. Every one of your interruptions delays the build by another ten minutes." The fact that developers and testers had come to me to ask for status updates was a symptom of a much larger problem that I didn't recognize at the time.

My calendar was booked with meetings all day long. Rarely did I get a chance to work uninterrupted until the evening or the weekend. Four months into the new job, I pulled an all-nighter in the office, working as fast as possible to catch up on the mountain of work. When the program manager arrived at 6:30 the next morning, he thought I had just arrived early. He was not pleased to hear that I was headed home to take a nap. Sleep deprivation was another red flag that I didn't give enough thought to at the time. Later on, after years spent working in technology, I recognized that relentless heroism—staying late night after night, wearing two hats, and consistently playing catch-up—is unsustainable. Quality doesn't happen on four hours of sleep.

We overload ourselves and we overload our teams—this is the everyday reality within the information technology sector. And, because we get interrupted all the time, we stop work on one task and start work on a different task, from one project to the next, never focusing on one thing long enough to do it justice. This *context switching* kills our ability to settle into work and concentrate sufficiently. As a result, we are unhappy with the quality of our work despite our desire for it to be good.

The problem is that we are working with dysfunctional processes—companies haven't adapted to keep up with demand in a healthy, sustainable way. Instead, we see the continued use of antiquated approaches meant to keep workers busy all the time. These processes are not working. This is the elephant in the office. If workers were able to get everything done right and on time, there wouldn't be an issue. But that's about as common as a black swan. The amount of requests (the demand) and the amount of time people have to handle the requests (their capacity) is almost always unbalanced. This is why we need a *pull system*—in which people can focus on one thing long enough to finish it before starting something new—like kanban. *Kanban* is a visual pull system based on *constraints* that allow workers to pull work when they have availability instead of work being pushed onto them regardless of their current workload. Since demand and capacity are frequently unbalanced, and it's almost impossible to get everything done on time, *systems* like kanban are for helping people balance all their work demand.

We'll get into kanban and where it fits into the process of making work visible a bit later, but for now, know that kanban is an approach to make work and problems visible and improve workflow efficiency. Kanban helps you get work done efficiently without burning the midnight oil night after night.

> "The aim of kanban is to make troubles come to the surface." —Taiichi Ohno

In the 2000s, I worked at an image licensing company in Seattle owned by Bill Gates called Corbis. I managed the Build and Configuration Management team.

We had a decent reputation among the Engineering department until 2005, when our two preproduction, seven-server environments quadrupled into eight preprod, twenty-five-server environments. We had seventeen databases. Each configured manually within the tightly coupled, highly dependent architecture. On top of that, the business asked us to develop new major systems at the same time, and they wanted the ability to deploy either one before the other. The dependencies between the existing system and the two new systems ballooned. My job grew from building out and managing twenty-five servers to building out and managing two hundred servers.

To deal with the changes, we created and maintained additional long living branches in *source control*, which is the place where developers check in their code for safe keeping. It was a terrible solution, but it helped the teams avoid clobbering each other's changes. Think of long living branches as a place where code is stored in isolation, where it's impossible to see the impact it might have on the code already released to production. It's kind of like adopting an older cat and praying that he and your current, much older cat will embrace each other with open paws. With more than two hundred servers to configure and maintain, configuration management was elevated. It took, at best, two weeks to restore production data to preproduction environments. We scheduled "M Is for Merge" days every six weeks, which consumed many developers' time.

Our reputation plunged. Developers complained that builds were taking too long. This, of course, offended me, and I set off to prove them wrong by collecting build-and-deploy time metrics.

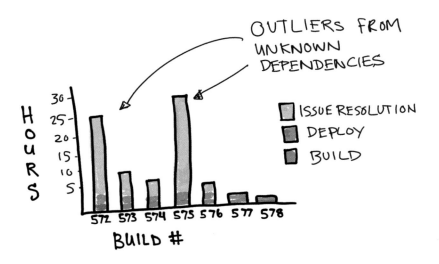

Figure 1. Builds Don't Take That Long

I pointed out that the big ball-of-mud architectural design disaster on our hands made deployment and maintenance of environments problematic. I pointed out that the manual *smoke tests* (tests to see if website functionality still works) delayed the time that developers and testers could see the latest changes and that lack of automated testing hurt our ability to quickly spot problems. Manual smoke tests were the norm. Both of these problems were dismissed fairly quickly as not real issues. The fact remained that developers and testers were unhappy. Business people were unhappy. And the boss was unhappy. It's no fun being on the team that "doesn't deliver." The barriers between teams were stronger than the connections. This is the problem with a bad system.

My own experience with a bad system coincided with the CFO deciding to replace the *enterprise resource planning (ERP)* system with another ERP product called SAP. An *ERP system* is a management information system which integrates things like planning, purchasing, inventory, sales, marketing, finance, and HR. SAP is its own ERP system, created by SAP AG, the fourth largest software company in the world.

My boss asked me, "Hey, do you want to manage the SAP Basis team as part of managing the build and release team?" Like an idiot, I said yes. I don't know how I could have possibly set myself up for more failure. I had zero experience with SAP, and adding SAP to my list of responsibilities spread me thin—to the point where I managed to be terrible at many different jobs. Multitasking is a good way to screw up progress, as I'm sure many of you reading this book know from experience.

At the time, I didn't know that all these things were red flags of a bad system. All I saw was that my performance was less than exemplary and that I was an unhappy employee who had started to consider other options.

I updated my resume.

In 2006, we spent a good deal of time analyzing and comparing different tools to manage our source code. Our team chose Team Foundation Server (TFS). We were a Microsoft shop, after all, and I ended up installing, configuring, and maintaining TFS—while also learning SAP, interviewing new candidates weekly, and helping to implement a new sustainment process. This process made it possible for us to deliver improvements every two weeks instead of every six months.

A user interface (UI) developer named Dwayne Johnson recognized the value in delivering small changes frequently and began socializing the idea of making small improvements on a consistent schedule. Dwayne started the process by fixing UI bugs on a regular bi-monthly cadence. At the time, it was just one more thing to support, but it was a very important one. These incremental and iterative improvements done on a regular cadence was our *Agile* alternative to traditional *Waterfall* development. These Agile methods wandered into our process, getting us thinking about a better approach to our work.

In April of '06, a Scottish Fellow from Microsoft appeared at Corbis. David Anderson visited us monthly to teach us how to apply the *Theory of Constraints (TOC)* to our work in exchange for permission to write a story about the Corbis Agile transformation. TOC is a way to identify the most important limiting factor (the constraint) that stands in the way of achieving a goal and then systematically improving that constraint until it is no longer the limiting factor. There was much excitement while reading his book *Agile Management for Software Engineering: Applying the Theory of Constraints for Business Results* as we thought we would do *Feature Driven Development*, a type of Agile development focused on cross-functional, collaborative, and *time-boxed* activities to build features. As Darren Davis writes in his blog "The Secret History of Kanban," David's methods "...eliminated explicit estimation from the process, and relied on data to provide a probabilistic means of determining when software was *likely* to be done."[2] David got us going on operations reviews and explained how important it is to measure progress (or lack thereof). Learning what to measure changed my world. Ranting didn't work, but measuring *cycle time* (the time it takes to do work) and presenting that data to leadership, did. I was able to influence leadership then and got buy-in to hire additional team members.

Sometimes the obvious gets lost in the crunch of the corporate world. We intuitively knew we had too many projects in flight, but it was hard to see until we measured the actual time that it took to get work done, at which point it became obvious the work spent more time in *wait states* than in work states. We spent time waiting for approval. Waiting for others to finish their part so we could start (or finish) our part. Waiting for uninterrupted time to focus on finishing the work. Waiting for the right time of day/week/month. And while we waited, we started something new, because, you know, with resource utilization as a goal, you have to stay busy *all* the time.

As Kate Murphy writes in her article "No Time to Think," "One of the biggest complaints in modern society is being overscheduled, over-committed and overextended. Ask people at a social gathering how they are and the stock answer is 'super busy,' 'crazy busy' or 'insanely busy.' Nobody is just 'fine' anymore."[3] I see evidence of this every day. When there is a still moment for reflective thought—say, while waiting for a meeting to begin—out come people's phones. Busyness can be an addiction for terminally wired ambitious people. But busyness does not equate to growth or improvement or value. Busyness often means just doing so many things at once that they all turn out crappy. Sometimes walking in the park and allowing ourselves time to think is the best way to seize the day. But horrors if an engineer sits idle for fifteen minutes simply thinking.

At Corbis, looking at the reasons why we worked on too many things at once was a revealing exercise. The CFO wanted to implement a new financial system. The SVP of Global Marketing wanted to blah, blah, blah. The VP of Media Services also wanted blah, blah, blah. The head of Sales wanted blah, blah, blah, *blah*. And they all wanted everything *now*. The resulting business priorities clashed all the way down the hierarchy and that was just the business side of the house. On the engineering side, not only did we need to implement all the business requests, we also had our own internal improvements to make and maintenance work to do. Furthermore, we still had to be available to drop everything when production issues occurred—like it or not, production comes first. The clashing priorities became apparent while looking at the many long-standing branched code lines, but other than that, there was no clear visual of the impact of working on too many things at once. It's hard to manage invisible work. With invisible work, we don't notice the explicit reminders that our mental budget is already full. There is no time to simply think.

After eight years at Corbis, I was one of forty-two people let go during the September 2008 round of layoffs. At this point, I decided to try something different. I got a job with AT&T Mobile on their program management team. But the regression from using the Lean kanban approach I helped create at Corbis to using a *Waterfall* approach (a traditional software development method where work waits until all the parts of the previous stage are complete), with estimations based off of time reports, was too much of a throwback for me. In July 2010, I fired myself.

In January 2011, David Anderson offered me the opportunity to research, develop, and teach a new course for David J. Anderson & Associates called Kanban for IT Operations. At the time, Europe led the United States in kanban implementations, so my research in February began in England, Sweden, and Germany. In March, we ran the first beta workshop in Boston, where I attended and spoke at DevOpsDays Boston 2011 at the Microsoft New England Research and Development Center in Boston.

Originally, I set off to write a reference for students to use during workshops while designing their kanban boards. Later, this piece grew into a time-saving reference for me as well. It became a place to capture not only everything I learned about applying Lean, kanban, and *flow* practices to my own work, but also selected equations, theories, and stats from thought leaders. For example, how to define Lean? For that, I prefer Niklas Modig and Pär Åhlström's definition. In their fantastic book *This Is Lean: Resolving the Efficiency Paradox*, they define *Lean* as, "a strategy of flow efficiency with key principles of just-in-time and visual management."[4]

So, what do we know? We know the demand for delivering business value to production, so that we can be competitive, is high. We know that many organizations are running deployment strategies that are slow and cumbersome. We also know that we are wired to do our best when we can clearly see what we are doing right as well as what we are doing wrong. This might seem obvious, but it's consistently ignored.

The technology world shows no signs of slowing down. The pace at which we need to deliver new capabilities to win new customers and prevent existing customers from walking away (*churn*) seems like warp speed. Many companies today are in survival mode, they just can't see it. This means that there is no better time than right now to elevate how we work. So, how do we level up our game?

The answer is straightforward and accessible. It doesn't cost you tons of money, and it doesn't take geniuses or specialists. All it takes is a shift from haphazardly saying yes to everything to deliberately saying yes to only the most important thing at that time. And to do it visually.

The solution is to design and use a workflow system that does the following five things:

1. Make work visible.
2. Limit work-in-progress (WIP).
3. Measure and manage the flow of work.
4. Prioritize effectively (this one may be a challenge, but stay with me—I'll show you how).
5. Make adjustments based on learnings from feedback and metrics.

What we will cover in this book:

- How to spot the five thieves that steal your time.
- How to expose the time thieves in order to make work visible and optimize *workflow.*
- How to know how you are really doing using metrics and feedback.
- What practices can get you into trouble.
- How to influence leadership decisions.

The examples described throughout the pages of this book are all based on my own real-life experiences and on those of others who have stood as witnesses to time-theft scenarios. Some prefer to avoid publicizing the crimes committed within their companies, so for them, the names have been changed to protect both the innocent and the guilty. We will also be looking at systemic organizational issues that must be addressed in order for you to be successful. As Edwards Deming said, "A bad system will beat a good person every time."[5]

This book is simultaneously an explanation, a how-to guide, and a business justification for using Lean, kanban, and flow methods to increase the speed and effectiveness of work.

Everything in this book may not apply to your specific situation. It has an IT bent to it, with several non-IT examples thrown in for good measure. Take what does apply to you and use the rest to gain insight into what people in other parts of your organization, or your competitors, might be dealing with. Each section in Part 2 includes exercises from my workshops, where we step through a series of activities designed to make work visible, improve workflow efficiency, and surface problems. They build upon each other, so it is best to read the sections in sequential order.

Explaining the concepts in this book to others should be a straightforward process. Getting buy-in to implement the suggested approaches may not be. Change is hard for humans. So, before we dive into workflow design, let's investigate exactly what prevents you from getting your work done quickly in the first place. Once we scrutinize the crimes committed against your existing workload, we can proceed with the insight and awareness necessary to do something about it. Let's get started.

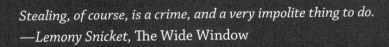

Stealing, of course, is a crime, and a very impolite thing to do.
—*Lemony Snicket,* The Wide Window

PART

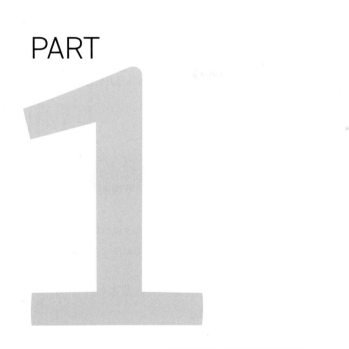

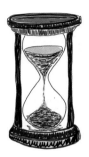

$$AVG\ CYCLE\ TIME = \frac{AVG\ WIP}{AVG\ THROUGHPUT}$$

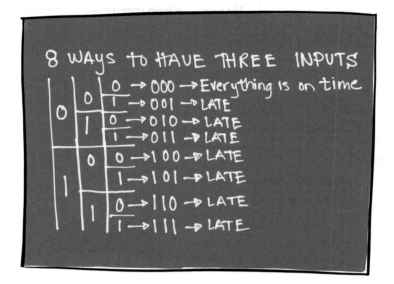

THE FIVE THIEVES OF TIME

If your wallet was stolen, you'd notice. If your security badge to your office was filched, you'd know it when you arrived. And if you opened the fridge to find your lunch missing, you'd make sure your office mates heard about it. So why don't people notice when they are robbed of something more valuable than their wallet, badge, or lunch—their nonrenewable time?

We grumble that there just aren't enough hours in the day and that someone else sure seems to have a lot of free time. But we regular mortals only have twenty-four hours in a day. The problem is that we don't protect our hours from being stolen. We allow thieves to steal time from us, day after day after day.

Who are these thieves of time?

The five thieves of time that prevent you from getting work done include:

1. **Too Much Work-in-Progress (WIP)**—Work that has started, but is not yet finished. Sometimes referred to as partially completed work.
2. **Unknown Dependencies**—Something you weren't aware of that needs to happen before you can finish.
3. **Unplanned Work**—Interruptions that prevent you from finishing something or from stopping at a better breaking point.
4. **Conflicting Priorities**—Projects and tasks that compete with each other. This is exacerbated when you are uncertain about what the most important thing is to do.
5. **Neglected Work**—Partially completed work that sits idle on the bench.

These five thieves hide right under your nose, comfortably cozy between you and your work. They leave clues at every crime scene. If we're going to get stuff done, we must trap these thieves to expose the crimes they commit. Once the thieves are caught, we can begin to do something about their insidious wreckage. Instead of being at their mercy, we can turn that dark corner, take back control, and make the kind of improvements that matter.

Beware the barrenness of a busy life.
—Socrates

1.1

TOO MUCH WORK-IN-PROGRESS (WIP)

On the roof of a building, Saturday, 9:00 a.m.

A man undertakes an item on his honey-do list (his to-do list, heavily influenced by his spouse), which includes dismantling the roof of an outbuilding. Over the years, this man's list of things to do has included repairing everything from appliances to septic systems. He has buried power lines, felled ninety-foot-tall cedar trees, and built cabins and garages step-by-step from excavating foundations to installing flooring, heating, plumbing, electricity, and roofing.

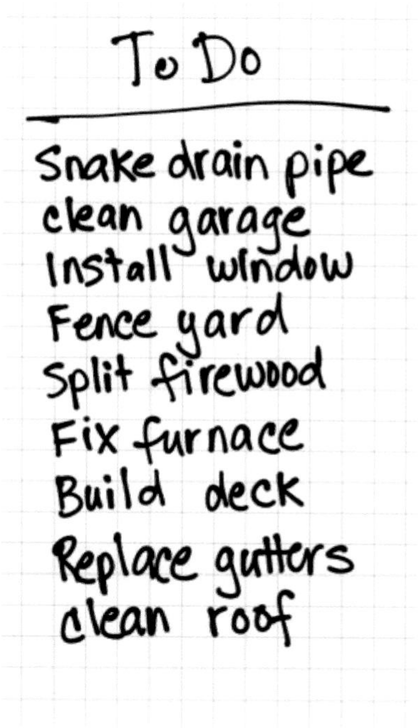

To Do

Snake drain pipe
clean garage
Install window
Fence yard
Split firewood
Fix furnace
Build deck
Replace gutters
clean roof

Recently, he seismically retrofitted an unreinforced, hollow-tile foundation. I am this man's assistant, which includes (but is by no means limited to) acting as tape measure holder, safety inspector, and demolition and cleanup crew. One day, while helping him tear down the rafters of an old, crumbling twenty-four-by-thirty-six foot outbuilding (I on the ground, he on the roof), I casually suggested that we build a sixteen-by-twenty-four-foot greenhouse on the back forty. From the top of the twenty-five-foot-tall rotting roof, my beloved husband looked at me incredulously and said, "Hon, can't you see I'm busy up here?!"

The tech sector does not have a monopoly on too much work to do. Talented people everywhere receive long to-do lists. The problem for a spouse who can build or fix anything is that the other spouse provides them with a long list of things to do. And it's hard for them to say no (unless they are atop a twenty-five-foot tall rotting roof).

We humans have a hard time saying no for a variety of reasons. Reason number one is because we like the person who asked us. The same holds true at the office. Because network engineer Sean gives me a heads up on work coming down the pipe that impacts me, I say he's nice and am willing to help him out when he needs something. But Carlos! Carlos knew about this port change two weeks ago and is only just now telling me at 5 p.m. on Friday?! My mental narrative says, "I don't really want to help you."

There are five other main reasons people give when I ask them, "Why do you take on more work than you have the capacity to do?"

1. **We are team players**—"I don't want to be the person who lets the team down."

2. **We fear humiliation**—"I don't want to be criticized or fired." Yes is easier to say than no—especially to the boss. Refusing a manager's request can be risky in some cultures.

3. **We like new and shiny**—It's much more fun than doing the grunt work it takes to finish something complicated and unglamorous.

4. **We don't realize how big the request is until we start working on it**—"Oh, no problem. I can get that done in just a couple of hours," but the task takes much longer.

5. **We like to please people.**—"I say yes to most requests in general because I want to be liked, admired, respected. "

Vanessa Bohns, social psychologist and professor of management sciences at the University of Waterloo in Ontario says, "It comes down to this fundamental motivation we have to stay connected to other people. We don't want to reject people. We don't want people to think poorly of us...so we are really managing the impressions other people have of us."[1] On the flip side, we rarely realize the power we have over other people when we ask them to do something, especially if others worry about explicit or perceived positions of power.

In textbook terminology, too much work-in-progress (WIP) is when the demand on the team exceeds the capacity of the team—which is a rather boring way to say that our teams are drowning in work, often because their schedule is completely full. Every minute of the day is fully scheduled (or fully allocated to 100% resource utilization). The most talented have the longest lists. This equates to people doing their full-time job on top of everything else that is expected of them, such as troubleshooting *environment issues* (problems with the configuration of servers that prevent website functionality and other things from working right), hiring new team members, and completing merit reviews, to name just a few. Similar to how our digestion system lets us know when we've stuffed too much food down it, Thief Too Much WIP attacks us if we cram too many meetings into our day, leaving us unable to begin the day's to-do list until 6:00 p.m.

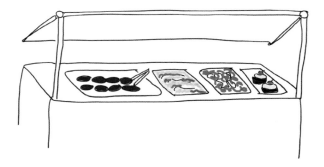

Why Too Much WIP Matters

Too much WIP matters for a number of reasons. It can result in many issues, including delayed delivery of value, increased costs, decreased quality, conflicting priorities, and irritable staff, to name a few. When we start a new task before finishing an older task, our WIP goes up and things take longer to do. So does the potential loss from things taking too long to complete and being unable to realize the value of it sooner. We measure this with cycle time. *Cycle time* is the amount of elapsed time that a *work item* spends as work-in-progress. In addition, business value that could have been realized sooner gets delayed because of too much WIP. This is known as *cost of delay*. It's a concept used to communicate value and urgency—a measure of the impact of time on the outcomes we want, such as customers buying our product this month instead of next month.

When you delay the delivery of a new feature because another request got bundled in with it, there's a cost for the delay of that new feature. It could mean late feedback, less profit, or a missed sales lead opportunity. Your new feature gets hijacked on its way to your customer, and the more stuff you add, the longer the customer waits. If customers wait too long, they shop elsewhere. Once customers give up and move on, you lose. Maybe it was worth it—but do you really know?

In general and for the purposes of this book, I define customers in two flavors:

External customers: People outside your organization who buy or use your product or service. If they move on to greener pastures, you lose revenue—and you risk a less-than-favorable review on your company's Facebook or Amazon page.

Internal customers: People inside your organization who ask you to do something or who consume your work. A Product Development team is a customer of the security engineer who detects vulnerabilities in the product or the platform it sits on. An employee is a customer of the manager who provides feedback. Internal customers impact WIP. For example, Help Desk WIP grows when the accounting admin gets locked out of his computer. Marketing team WIP grows when the technical evangelist adds a new conference to her tour. Platform Operations WIP grows when the VP of whatever hires a third-party vendor to build a new integration.

WIP is a leading indicator of cycle time. The more items that are worked on at the same time, the more doors open up that allow dependencies and interruptions to creep in. Trailing or lagging indicators are backward focused—they measure performance data already captured. Most metrics measured in technology and business, such as *lead time* (the elapsed time it takes to complete a request from the time it was first requested), cycle time, and *throughput* (the number of things completed over a period of time), are trailing indicators. That is, we don't know how long certain things will take something until those things are completed.

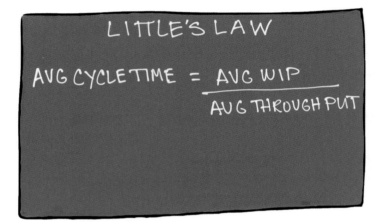

There is a relationship between the amount of WIP and cycle time—it's called Little's Law, where the average cycle time for finishing tasks is calculated as the ratio between WIP and throughput. WIP is a primary factor in the equation. It's obvious when you think about it—as soon as you get on a clogged freeway you know that your commute is going to take longer. For this reason, Thief Too Much WIP is the ringleader of all the other thieves.

You know Thief Too-Much-WIP is stealing time from you when:

Context switching is common: When computers context switch, the state of the process currently being executed is saved so that when it is rescheduled, the state can be restored to its correct spot. Because computers perform hundreds of context switches per second, it's easy to believe that multiple tasks are performed in parallel, when in reality the central processing unit (CPU) is actually alternating or rotating between tasks at high speed. As Todd Watts writes in his blog post "Addressing the Detrimental Effects of Context Switching with DevOps," the overhead incurred by a context switch, managing the process of storing and restoring the state, negatively impacts operating system (OS) and application performance.[2] Because a context switch can involve changing a large amount of data, it can be one of the most costly operations in an OS.[3]

Just like computers, humans incur overhead when context switching between different tasks. Although with humans, the overhead is much higher. Data structures containing all the information registers and OS-specific data, along with the exact point of entry for where to resume the process, aren't automatically rescheduled in the brain like they are in a CPU. Context switching in computers has a programmable flow to it.

The notion of flow in humans doesn't happen when context switching is the norm. Flow is the concept of focused motivation. It's characterized by complete absorption in what one does (energized focus). It's an optimal state that results in high levels of productivity and satisfaction. To achieve flow is to be in the zone—that space where intrinsic motivation and creativity flourish.

To achieve flow, a focused concentration on the task at hand is necessary. This doesn't happen when distractions, whether in the form of email, food, coworkers, or social media, interrupt us. When we are responsible for multiple things, such as maintaining production and delivering new features, we shift what we're doing based on perceived priorities. By the time we get back to working on whatever we were doing before the interruption, we have to start all over again. Flow requires a "do not disturb" ethos.

Your customers wait for long periods of time: Flow also requires a level of efficiency. When it comes to *flow efficiency*, the length of time you keep your customer waiting is of prime consideration. If new projects are started before existing projects are finished, work piles up, requiring more resources and/or more people. It is inefficient from a customer perspective to prioritize starting new work over finishing the things you have already begun. If I'm writing a blog about kanban and the next step in the process is to have it edited by someone on the Marketing team, then beginning a new blog about DevOps before incorporating Marketing's edits for the kanban blog means I'll have to deal with a context switch when the editor gets back to me.

Quality suffers: Quality suffers from too much WIP. When I was at Corbis and took on the additional role of managing the new SAP basis team, I shot myself in the foot. I had to learn a complicated mainframe product while building a new team on top of continuing to do my original job. I hadn't done anything with mainframes since my first job out of college seventeen years before, and I didn't know anything about SAP. I didn't take the time to learn it very well because I had all these other things that had to be done on my plate. The result was a predictable one in retrospect: Neither the team nor

SAP nor my other responsibilities got adequate attention. This led to a poorly managed team and an irritated me.

Irritated staff: Context switching is irritating—you're rarely left with enough time to do a good job, nor with sufficient space to master the task or skill. Harry F. Harlow, an American psychologist, says in Daniel Pink's book *Drive*, "The joy is in the pursuit more than the realization. In the end, mastery attracts precisely because mastery eludes."[4] Mastery eludes because there is insufficient time to pursue something long enough and deep enough before being interrupted.

Interruptions thwart deep thinking. Sherlock Holmes thinks best when he goes to his "mind palace" in the BBC adaptation of Conan Doyle's famous sleuth's escapades.[5] Using a mental technique called the method of loci (Latin for location), he travels to his memory bank, a sort of mental map where memories are deposited, to withdraw memories. But he needs an environment void of distractions and interruptions, and he gets quite cranky if others interfere with his mind palace. And with good cause—it's downright irritating to be interrupted when deep in thought. Time thieves love the area of deep thought because, as David Rock relates in his book *Your Brain at Work: Strategies for Overcoming Distraction, Regaining Focus, and Working Smarter All Day Long*, it can take up to twenty minutes to get back to that same thinking spot after an interruption.[6]

Someone asks you if you have five minutes and you say yes: All too often, when someone asks you, "Do you have five minutes?" and you say yes, you end up working late. It's annoying and sometimes exhausting, and we do it to ourselves. Even though I teach this stuff, I fall into this trap too. In our defense, we do get more endorphins from saying yes[7]—enough that even grouchy people want to say yes.

However, it's not productive to say yes all the time, nor is it sustainable to consistently work evenings and weekends. The power of kanban gives you the freedom to finish work.

Kanban is Japanese for signal card—a card that, very simply, signals your availability to do some work. When you pull a card from the backlog onto the in-progress area of your kanban board, you commit to being available to do the work that the card represents.

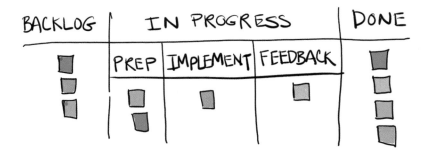

Figure 2. Prep Implement Feedback Board

The number of cards under the in-progress area reveals the amount of WIP on the kanban board. The board in Figure 2 shows a WIP of four. WIP limits are what make kanban a pull system. When a card is finished, it signals available capacity and causes another card to be pulled into In Progress. Work flows across the board based on the WIP limits and pull policies. If WIP limits are set appropriately, the system cannot become overloaded. The WIP limit is what allows you to say, "No, there is no capacity to take on more work right now." Think of reducing WIP not as limiting but as liberating. The right amount of WIP is what enables us to maintain a healthy amount of work.

When you say to your pal, "Yes, I'll do that," you have just authorized and prioritized "that" request over all the other requests in the backlog. Dan Weatbrook, Tableau WebOps Manager, calls this "born-in-doing"—a way of cutting in line, if you will.[8] It's a thief stealing time away from previous requests and is one reason why requests in the backlog take so long (and sometimes never make it) to the In Progress state.

These elements of too much WIP crop up across all the thieves. Thief Too Much WIP is the ringleader, and the other thieves steal ideas from this relentless troublemaker. We will get into more details on how the thieves interact with each other a bit later. For now, let's take stock of what we've covered so far about our thieving ringleader and move on to thief number two, Thief Unknown Dependencies.

KEY TAKEAWAYS

- We have a tendency to say yes to any request, regardless of how busy we are.

- Too much WIP prevents us from completing work on time, causes quality to suffer, increases costs, and irritates staff.

- Work-in-progress and cycle time have a relationship. High WIP means that other items sit idle, waiting for attention longer.

- Context switching, which wastes time, is a major consequence of too much WIP.

- We must learn to say no to additional work when our schedules are full.

The definition of freedom is that there is no dependency.
—Dada Bhagwan

1.2

UNKNOWN DEPENDENCIES

A friend of mine works for a company with $23 billion in yearly revenue, where Product Team X deployed a component that broke Team Y's product. Now, Team Y's customers have to fork out $5 million for the new Y part. This is on top of the $10 million that they just paid to buy a new X part because the old X part was at the end of its life and was no longer supported. The customers in this scenario used parts created by both the X and Y teams. Part Y needed part X to function correctly. The only way Team Y's customers could get their needs met was to buy the new X part.

Now this company has a major public relations disaster on their hands. They are losing significant market share because the two product teams didn't talk to each other. Team Y had zero visibility into Team X's decision to release a new version of software that Team Y's product was dependent on. The blame game, replete with finger pointing, begins and now a VP's head is on the chopping block. It's very expensive when teams are unaware of mutually critical information. This is the type of thing that happens when there are unknown dependencies.

Let's define *dependency*. From my perspective, when we talk about dependencies, three types emerge:

1. **Architecture (both software and hardware)**—where change in one area can break another area (i.e., cause it to stop functioning)
2. **Expertise**—where counsel or aid from a person with specific know-how is needed to do something
3. **Activity**—Where progress cannot be made until an activity is complete

If your manager is stuck in a meeting and thus you can't get the go-ahead to register for the conference before the day is out, then you've got yourself a dependency. Another example would be waiting on a test environment or a database restore from production before you are able to move your work forward.

Tightly coupled software architecture is a victim of the big bully that is Thief Unknown Dependencies. When a decision to remove a table from a database negatively impacts another team, Thief Unknown Dependencies scores big time. This is an example of a software code dependency.

Specialized expert skill-sets are at risk of being hit by this big bully thief. A developer wonders, "Are there unknown vulnerabilities in this code?" while waiting on feedback from a security expert. But the security expert is busy discovering how someone hacked into their now unsecure database. A question waits on input from a database architect. "Is the data in the test environment wrong? Can they please check it out?" But the database architect is busy helping the security expert. When you are the only one on the team with a special skill set, you can be the bottleneck pulled in many directions. Expert skills in high demand are often unavailable when you need them. Thief Unknown Dependency snickers in delight.

A similar problem occurs for changes outside of your control in the form of third-party vendors. Major cloud providers, like Amazon EC2, Microsoft Azure, and Google Compute Engine, provide service-level agreement policies that guarantee their customers 99.95% uptime. This equates to twenty-two minutes of allowable downtime per month. When your cloud provider is down, you are down, and Thief Unknown Dependency laughs at you. Granted, your cloud provider is a known dependency, but do you always know it when they first strike? How much time does the team spend troubleshooting a problem before they realize it was the cloud provider who did it in the datacenter with the candlestick? But you still lose even if it's the provider's fault because you are constrained by contractual agreements. You may be compensated with time credits, but if a failure occurs, how much time is wiped out trying to recover lost data? If you totaled the hours a team troubleshoots an incident like this, how much time is really stolen?

Why Dependencies Matter

"Every dependency doubles your chance of being delayed or late."
— Troy Magennis

Troy Magennis gave an enlightening talk on dependencies at the Agile 2015 Conference in Washington, D.C. Troy uses basic *boolean logic* (where all values are either true or false) to show that there is only ever one possible combination of inputs that result in an on-time delivery. Every time you remove one dependency, half of the total possible delay combinations are removed. If delivery requires every piece being complete, every dependency you remove doubles your chances of delivering on time.[1]

Take a look at this example. If there are two inputs needed to deliver something, then there is only one chance in four of delivering on time. One chance in 2^n is the formula that computes the total number of binary permutations.

Come on now—math is fun! You got this. A binary digit can only be a 0 or a 1. A permutation is a way in which a number of things can be arranged. A binary permutation, then, is an arrangement of binary numbers. 2n is 2 to the power of n. When the number of inputs is two, n = 2, and we have 2 × 2, which equals 4, or 2 2.

Let's write them all down to see how it works. There are four ways to have two inputs.

If there are three inputs needed to ship, then there is only a one in eight chance of on-time delivery.

8 WAYS to HAVE THREE INPUTS
0 → 000 → Everything is on time
1 → 001 → LATE
0 → 010 → LATE
1 → 011 → LATE
0 → 100 → LATE
1 → 101 → LATE
0 → 110 → LATE
1 → 111 → LATE

Just by removing the strict delivery dependency, you double the chances (from one in eight to one in four) of on-time delivery. There will always only be a single chance where everything is on time.

Imagine you have reservations for dinner with four people who travel independently to a fine dining restaurant and you're told you won't be seated until all four people arrive. There are sixteen possible outcomes.

That is to say, sixteen possible combinations for whether people arrive on time or not. If you chart that out, fifteen outcomes have at least one person arriving late and only one outcome where everyone arrives on time. Dependencies are asymmetrical in their impact. With four dependencies, it's not a 25% probability you won't be seated, it's a 93% (15/16th) probability that you won't be seated. There's a much greater chance that fifteen out of sixteen times, someone will be late. Time to call it a night and hit up the burger joint.

Figure 3, a three dependency chart, helps to visualize this math for three dependencies where the probability is 12.5% of being seated on time. When you add one more dependency, the probability is just one in sixteen, or .06% probability. Unless, that is, they work in Operations—then they'll never leave work early enough to arrive on time.

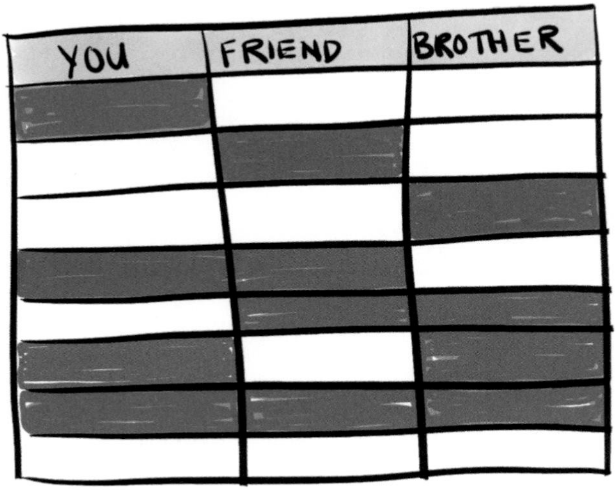

Figure 3. Three Dependency Chart

You know Thief Unknown Dependency is stealing time from you when:

- Coordination needs are high, and project managers run around trying to get everyone aligned.
- People aren't available when you need them.
- A change in one part of the code/outline/plan unexpectedly changes something else.

When the local pizza company delivers more than two pizzas to the same meeting room, pay attention. A two-pizza team is a team that can be fed with just two pizzas—about five to seven people depending on the size of the appetite. If three two-pizza teams need to have a joint meeting to discuss their dependencies on each other, then you have high coordination costs. Fifteen to twenty-one people bantering their point of view can consume a lot of time. When was the last time fifteen people agreed on anything? When coordination needs are high, people aren't available when you need them to be.

Small teams can move fast. Nothing beats a small, cohesive group of people who communicate and collaborate effectively. The problem occurs when dependencies span across teams, causing things to break. When one team breaks another team's functionality by creating incompatible changes, the impacts can be destructive, as mentioned in the opening of this section about my friend's $23 billion company. When we attempt to increase the performance of individual teams by breaking them down into smaller groups, hidden dangers await if there are unknown dependencies.

Cross team communication is hard. When a bunch of two-pizza teams with lots of dependencies between them spend a lot of time coordinating to avoid stepping on each other's code (due to the merging of the different teams' code branches), the benefit of the small team diminishes. Smaller teams can increase integration costs. We like small teams because they can move fast. Just realize that by moving fast as an individual team, you may be paying the price of not moving very fast as a whole organization.

Lastly, remember the following common attributes from Thief Too Much WIP: costly context switching and expensive interruptions. Distraction is one of the biggest hurdles to high-quality knowledge work, costing almost one trillion dollars annually.[2]

- It's expensive when teams are unaware of mutually critical information.

- Architecture, expertise, and activities on hold are some of the common dependencies you might run into.

- Every dependency increases the probability you will be late. If possible, reduce dependencies to save time and money and avoid other complications. Conversely, every dependency you can find and eliminate doubles your chances of delivering on time.

- When coordination needs are high, people aren't available when you need them. The same is true for experts—when demand for a skill is high, experts are unavailable.

- When it comes to dependencies, individual team performance can increase to the detriment of company-wide performance.

○ ○ ○ ○ ○

Code will be used in ways we cannot anticipate, in ways it was never designed for, and for longer than it was ever intended.
—Joshua Corman

1.3

UNPLANNED WORK

Downtown, USA, Tuesday Morning

Picture this: A senior business executive sees business value in an integration between her company's product and another software application. He hires a third party to integrate a new service and promises zero impact to her Product Development teams.

The external, offshore team designs an integration but overlooks the fast growth of the user base, resulting in an overburdened database. The database server revolts, setting off alerts to the duty pager. Operations staff have to stop work on a high priority task to troubleshoot the angry database. Two cups of coffee and two hours later, the issue is resolved, and people can get back to work on that high-priority task they were deep into before the interruption occurred...right after their meeting that starts in ten minutes. This was not the intent of the senior business executive.

People were interrupted and pulled away from important work. The interruption (the unplanned work) caught people off guard. It was an unintended consequence of a move by a well-meaning executive which negatively impacted high-priority work, work that will now be delayed because of the interruption. The time spent away from working on the original priority is irreversibly wiped out. This is the problem with unplanned work—it sets back planned work. It increases uncertainty in the system and makes the system less predictable as a result.

Sometimes unplanned work comes in the form of a necessary strategic change in direction: "Let's stop marketing to everyone and just focus on large enterprises." But often, unplanned work comes in the form of unnecessary rework or expedited work requests. These are the fires that stem from some failure. Demand from failure is called, predictably, *failure demand*, and it is a frequent target for Thief Unplanned Work. It can be the case, though, that a dependency from a team just down the hall from you is a greater risk to not responding to your needs. This usually results in a communication up your line of command to the common denominator leader and then back down the food chain to the person responsible, resulting in an interruption/delay to that person's lunch (hopefully, it's still in the fridge).

 Let me be clear, I am not suggesting all work should be preplanned. It is irresponsible (maybe even delusional), to believe that it's possible to know everything up front while planning a complex project. Quite the contrary—we don't know much about what we don't yet know. Sometimes changes in direction are necessary, because

new information emerges as we work to solve problems. A major value of the Agile movement is to encourage responding to change over following a plan. Life is uncertain. Change is inevitable. It's a law—the second law of thermodynamics to be precise.

Why Unplanned Work Matters

Unplanned and expedited work steals time away from work that's creating value. The *2016 State of DevOps Report* survey data show that high performers are able to spend 28% more time on planned work.[1] Unplanned work is considered a measure of quality because the more unplanned work, the less time for creating value. "All hands on deck" incidents tend to reduce performance and increase variability.

As mentioned above, unplanned work steals time away from planned work. However, there are times when it is understandable and necessary for unplanned work to muscle its way to the front of the priority *queue*. If the request happens to be, "Please look into why no one can log in to the website," then you really have no choice but to drop what you're doing to fix the issue. Unpredictable fluctuations in demand can reduce the ability to deliver things as expected.

You know Thief Unplanned Work is stealing time from you when urgent issues pull people away from focused efforts on creating value. This could manifest in anything from an unexpected fire drill to a malfunction with a heavily used program that then adds uncertainty and variability into our everyday work. Because of this interruption, something else is going to take longer than expected. If the work is frequently late, chances are Thief Unplanned Work (i.e., failure demand or strategic change in direction) is stealing not only your time but also your predictability.

The reality is that we work in webs of interdependencies. The complexity of human interactions consistently produces things that no one wants. Thief Unplanned Work is a mainstay in a complex world where change and uncertainty flourish.

Unplanned work not only causes its own problems but brings with it all the problems of too much WIP: context switching, interruptions, delayed work, and increased cost. When unplanned work (such as fixing broken functionality on a website) creeps into the everyday work scene, it increases the amount of work already sitting on your plate. The more urgent unplanned work that interrupts your day, the bigger the pileup of partially completed planned work. The relationship between unplanned work and too much WIP is a twisted, codependent liaison resulting in heaps of unexpected work that is impossible to catch up on. Unless you keep stepping up, planned responsibilities fall behind. Overfunctioning becomes an automatic response, eventually becoming dysfunctional and imbalanced. That's why it is so important to learn to identify and tackle, as early and often as possible, the issues that Thief Unplanned Work creates.

Unplanned work increases risk, uncertainty, reduces predictability, and smacks down morale. But that doesn't mean we have to simply lay there and let Thief Unplanned Work walk all over us. There are ways we can fight back.

Making work visible is a core component in combating thieves like Thief Unplanned Work and is also a core component of kanban, the system that we will come back to again and again throughout this book. Kanban cards show all kinds of information that traditionally have been hard to see. Kanban cards live on kanban boards, and kanban boards answer questions like, "What is being worked on?"

and "What state is the work in?" and "Who's doing what?" All essential information is visible on the board, so you don't have to chase down workers to ask them what is happening and you don't have to wait for a politically sanitized weekly status report to get a glimpse of transparency.

KEY TAKEAWAYS

- Unplanned work adds unpredictability to the system.
- It's all about predictability and expectations. Unplanned work eats expectations for breakfast.
- High-performing companies spend less time working on unplanned work than lower performing companies.
- Sometimes we have no choice but to drop current projects to focus on urgent unplanned work.
- Unplanned work steals time away from planned work.
- Unplanned work is hard to see, but it can be made visible. Kanban helps to combat and better anticipate unplanned work by making work visible.
- Plan for unplanned work by reserving capacity for when it arrives.

Focus is a matter of deciding what things you're not going to do.
—*John Carmack*

1.4

CONFLICTING PRIORITIES

Imagine a room of forty-one IT Operations engineers working for a successful gaming company. They are smart. They are engaged. They are well paid. On occasion, Nerf gun darts zoom across the room. All appears to be thriving. Except that when you stand back and observe the room a bit longer, you notice things that don't look right.

The team's poorly attended *stand-ups* (a fifteen-minute meeting where team members check in with each other to discuss what's preventing them from moving forward) held every day, include more foot shuffling than discussion. The VP of Operations jokes half-heartedly about another trip to the CEO's office as if he were being called to see the Principal. People wearing anxious expressions frequently approach the two project managers' area. The anxious people are business product owners who want status updates on their projects. It turns out the only way they can get visibility on their projects is through the project managers, but the two managers are busy planning capacity and procuring hardware. That list is jotted down on sticky notes and in notepads and on calendar tasks—in other words, it is spread out over many different list-making tools.

The project managers facilitate a daily stand-up in front of a seventy-two-inch plasma screen mounted on the wall. Seeking clarity, they open the floor to the Operations team, asking them to identify blocked work and other issues preventing them from finishing tasks. The project managers' hope is that they will be able to help remove project impediments and provide accurate status updates to the product owners. But when the project managers ask the Operations engineers if anyone is blocked, the Ops people return blank stares and silence, because they don't want to point fingers or get a team member in trouble. The issues causing the blockages are invisible to the project managers.

This is a familiar scene on any given day at organizations where stand-ups go wrong. The engineers are trying to get clarity on priorities from the project managers, and the project managers are trying to get clarity on statuses from the Operations engineers. In both cases, the common denominator is unclear priorities. Invisible work and invisible priorities hamper the alignment needed among engineers, project managers, and business people to make effective progress. Again, it all comes back to the necessity of making work visible for everyone.

However, for many, there is confusion on what real progress looks like. A team of engineers who look really busy but who are not completing project features are a red flag. Having a bunch of projects that are sitting at 90% complete does the company no good. Sales can't sell a feature to a customer if the customer cannot access the feature; features are only valuable if customers can use them.

Going back to the same daily stand-up, in the top left-hand corner of the plasma screen is a list of the Operations team's top four priorities:

capacity expansion, disaster recovery, security, and site reliability. The assumption is that, given these priorities, the team can prioritize their own work.

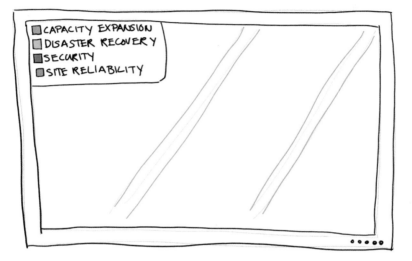

Of the thirty-three projects that this team of forty-one engineers is working on, more than half of them are identified as priority one. Yet, no one is willing to point out that the team is being asked to do too many projects at one time. And no one is paying attention to the metrics that show just how long work is sitting queued up, waiting for someone to become available to do the work. The careless implication is that *all* the projects must get done now. The team believes they are doing everything in their power to get all the work done, yet many of the thirty-three projects remain incomplete, and new projects are started before existing projects are finished.

We've all encountered situations like this in varying contexts: group projects in middle school in which no one yet knows how to prioritize, unreasonable deadlines set by managers who want all the work done "yesterday," and/or trying to multitask through your to-do list by tackling everything at once instead of accomplishing tasks by level of value.

The negative impact of copious untracked dependencies, lengthy cycle times, and habitual overtime is invisible in the short term. Eventually, though, network errors, security oversights, and missed delivery dates become uncomfortably visible. What's not happening here is the acknowledgment that some of these projects should be set aside until the teams have capacity.

Why Conflicting Priorities Matter

"Productivity isn't about being a workhorse, keeping busy, or burning the midnight oil.... It's about priorities and fiercely protecting your time."
— Margarita Tartakovsky

Thief Conflicting Priorities cackles with delight when people are uncertain or disagree on what to work on.

Say a team was working on a report that took ages to complete. Not only did it take a long time, but it was also delivered six months later than leadership wanted. Let's say we examined the team's workload, and it turns out they had thirteen initiatives, which was more than the number of people they had on the whole team. Furthermore, their priority meetings took longer than an hour and happened every week. If we reduce this team's initiatives to, say, seven, they now have better focus and their priority meetings are shorter. Reducing the volume of WIP helps people prioritize more effectively because there are fewer things vying for attention. Lest we forget that Thief Too Much WIP is the ringleader of all the thieves, one cause of too much WIP is the failure to prioritize properly.

If people can't prioritize effectively, they try to do too much at once and everything takes longer. Then, too much WIP equals longer cycle times, which leads to delays in delivering value to customers. Happy customers (whether internal or external) brighten our day and our pocketbooks. Longer cycle times delay the opportunity to receive vital feedback from customers about our work, which in turn creates a crevice for more thievery to sneak in.

If everything is priority one, then nothing is a priority one, and everything takes too long. As Ross Garber says, "Many things may be important, but only one can be the most important."[1] It could be that the greatest value for the business today would be for you to go help someone else finish something instead of starting something new.

You know that Thief Conflicting Priorities is stealing time from you when you hear people ask/say:
- "When will my thing be done?"
- "My thing is a high priority!"
- "If my thing doesn't get done by _____, then..."

Another indicator conflicting priorities are bogging down your work is when you find yourself spending countless hours in meetings discussing priorities. Thief Conflicting Priorities is a close cousin of Thief Unplanned Work. And just like unplanned work, heaps of older, planned work pile up when priorities conflict. When today's highest priority work supersedes yesterday's highest priority work, look to the ringleader Thief Too Much WIP as the core problem. Teams will fall behind on planned responsibilities unless they keep stepping up.

KEY TAKEAWAYS

- There is one most important thing—let people know what it is.

- Conflicting priorities occur when people are uncertain on what the highest priority is.
This leads to too much WIP, which leads to longer cycle times.

- Conflicting priorities that compete for the same people and resources block flow and increase partially completed work.

- What we see as a priority frequently clashes with what others see as a priority.

In delay, there lies no plenty.
—*William Shakespeare,* Twelfth Night

1.5

NEGLECTED WORK

When I was with Corbis, we relied on an ERP application called JD Edwards (JDE). It was an old, customized version and quite fragile. Taking JDE offline to do backups or database restores impacted the accounts payable and accounts receivable functions, and applying a new JDE upgrade from the vendor broke the customized database tables. So, we did what many IT shops surprisingly do—thought short term and continued using the ten-year-old unsupported version. What could possibly go wrong? Well, the manual JDE build-and-deploy process routinely overwrote configuration files during deployments, causing new orders to disappear. Eventually, everyone became afraid to touch the JDE server, and as a result, it was left alone for the better part of ten years, until we replaced it with SAP. In some ways, aging software is much like an older car that needs regular oil changes and tune-ups to keep it functioning correctly. Old software in itself is not a problem. Old software that is not maintained and is not part of an automated build, test, and deploy process is a problem.

Maintenance of legacy systems is one of the most neglected types of work. Old, fragile systems decay, making them unpredictable as the technical debt adds up. The entropy of an isolated system always increases over time. If not repaired or replaced, the system eventually bombs, blocking or delaying something important. This consumes time and energy, taking people away from other important work. "If it hurts, do it more often," as the saying goes. Frequency reduces difficulty. Until that principle is applied to system maintenance, the neglected work will remain a problem. When new requests continuously jump over or bypass important maintenance work, neglected work sits alone, sadly, like a rejected child at a lunch table in the school cafeteria.

Thief Neglected Work often plants invisible technical debt in the system, knowing that short-term thinking sways prioritization in favor of new features over protecting valuable assets. Like financial debt, *technical debt* incurs interest payments, which come in the form of extra effort required to fix software bugs and develop new features. Conflicting priorities and neglected work are also close cousins. (I imagine you're sensing a pattern here.) Neglected work doesn't get the attention, the budget, or the resources needed to be successful, like that ten-year-old JDE configuration that was still using a customized version of a no longer supported version. The impact of this aged and neglected system on our Corbis team was failure demand that occurred when the configuration files incorrectly pointed to the wrong instance. This was a high maintenance problem and cause for many a troubleshooting ticket.

If I had to identify what kind of work is most neglected, it would be the work related to improving quality, including deferred maintenance, bugs, technical debt, and code without tests (legacy software, as defined by Michael Feathers).[1] Time and cost often win when it comes to getting product out the door ("Just skip those tests. We need to get this delivered. We'll come back to it later."). The current corporate culture that focuses on people being "busy" all the time is absurd. Work is neglected when people are "busy." Busy people, however, do not signal productivity—delivered value does.

Two significant areas where work stalls include work waiting on feedback and work deemed important but not urgent. A third factor is what Donald Reinertsen termed "zombie projects."[2] Zombie projects are low-value projects that are barely alive. They lurk around looking for handouts, but they get no love. They are starving for money, resources, and people.

Nevertheless, they persist, and in doing so, these starving projects subtly siphon people's time and energy away from higher value projects. When you discover a zombie project, kill it. Kill it so the more important work will be delivered sooner and with fewer interruptions.

Some people have difficulty killing projects that have started because of a desire to avoid losing whatever time and money have already been sunk into the project. The more people invest in a project, the harder it becomes to abandon it, even when a more rational decision based off of future value would be better. This is known as *sunk cost fallacy*. In *The Principles of Product Development Flow*, Donald Reinertsen suggests we should only consider the incremental investment needed to finish the project in comparison to its economic return.[3] Purging low-value jobs from the work queue makes sense whenever a surplus of high-value jobs is in progress. In other words, it's okay to kill zombie projects. If they are really needed, zombie projects can return from the dead. The things that matter most must not be sidetracked by the things that matter least.

However, zombie projects are not the only cause of neglected work. Businesses frequently prioritize new feature releases over fixing technical debt. They choose to work on revenue-generating work instead of revenue-protection work.

This rarely works out as the business hopes, particularly as problems discovered during the final stages of uncompleted projects drag engineers away from the newer projects. Because new work is started at a faster rate than partially completed work already in the pipeline is finished, the work piles up and takes longer to do (Thief Too Much WIP sneaking its way in again). Flow time metrics start to increase. It's like rush hour traffic. When more cars are entering the freeway than are leaving the freeway, drivers are greeted with a longer commute. And like the traffic jam on the freeway, the ensuing barrage of constant interruptions can bring workflow to a grinding halt.

Why Neglected Work Matters

Important work sits waiting until it eventually becomes an emergency or it causes distractions and interruptions. Neglected work is perishable. It ages. And like rotten fruit, it's wasteful. Fruit is expensive, consumes space on the countertop, and gets old and moldy and smells bad. And who wants that?

You know Thief Neglected Work is stealing time from you when you delay important tasks that will eventually become emergencies. It's like planning to take your better half out for your anniversary dinner, then deciding to skip going out this year in favor of batching it up with next year's anniversary. How do you think that would go over? If your partner would give you an earful about it, your neglected work will give you two.

Shining a light on how long work sits neglected is a useful exercise to undergo in order to understand the relationship between old work (think zombie projects) and newer, competing projects. Similar to all the other thieves, Thief Neglected Work is cheered on by Thief Too Much WIP.

KEY TAKEAWAYS

- If not dealt with, important neglected work eventually becomes an emergency.
- Beware of invisible technical debt accruing while teams are sidetracked by short-term priorities.
- Acknowledge zombie projects. Consider the impact they have on completing high-value projects. Either give them the attention they need or kill them.

Time is what we want most, but what we use worst.
—William Penn

PART

HOW TO EXPOSE
TIME THEFT TO
OPTIMIZE WORKFLOW

There is a reason our schools and offices are plastered with white-boards. We acquire more information through vision than through all the other senses combined.[1] Of the 100 billion neurons in our brains, approximately 20% are devoted to analyzing visual informa-tion.[2] The visual-spatial learner thinks primarily in images. A study done by psychologist and founder of the Institute for the Study of Advanced Development, Linda Kreger Silverman, suggests that two-thirds of the population have a visual-spatial preference.[3] The left hemisphere is sequential, analytical, and time-oriented. The right hemisphere perceives the whole, synthesizes, and apprehends movement in space. For visual-spatial learners, if the right hemisphere is not activated and engaged, then attention will be low and learning will be poor.

Unfortunately, unlike the visual transparency of physical labor, knowledge work takes place in the cerebral cortex of the brain, where thoughts are the result of signals passing through neurons on their way to the nervous system. Tucked away out of sight of coworkers, teammates, and the boss, our ideas for how to solve problems and design systems remain invisible to the rest of the world. How fantastic would it be if we could physically display all the intense mental labor that goes into creative problem-solving or conceptualizing new ideas with the click of a mouse or stroke of a dry erase pen ("See, boss, I really am working!")? While it may not be quite that easy, it is possible to achieve visibility of work in the technology sector by making those ideas, the state of the knowledge work, and the related problems visually accessible to ourselves and to those impacted.

When we bring our visual sense to solving problems, we get clarity around the problem, and it's easier to make decisions. Making work visible is one of the most fundamental things we can do to improve our work because the human brain is designed to find meaningful patterns and structures in what is perceived through vision.

Thus, it makes sense that when we can't see our work, we have a hard time managing it. But, while this seems obvious, it's not something we think about. We tend to ignore the mundane, the things that are so intrinsic we don't even notice that they are there. This is an illusion of simplicity.

I would like to change the dialogue on this illusion and call this "obvious thing" an elegant visual—a beautiful visual that provides utility by depicting the flow of work and improving communication. An intuitive visual that is not only useful but also relevant, and therefore interesting to gaze upon. The better the visual, the more value. An elegant visual appeals to the senses and captures the interest of the onlooker.

In Part 2, we'll be sharing real-world problems, examples, and exercises for designing a flow-based system that brings clarity to priorities and visibility to risks, and liberates you from the advancing blitz of too much work. In Part 3, we look at systemic organizational issues that will need to be addressed in order for you to be successful.

In doing so, we will be focusing on the system that efficiently and effectively addresses and manages the core issues caused by the five thieves by making work visible and smoothing out workflow: Lean kanban flow. As stated in the introduction, the rest of this book is simultaneously an explanation, a how-to guide, and a business justification for seeing work flow fast by using Lean, kanban, and flow methods.

Section 2.1 is for readers who want a lesson on how to get started with using kanban and for those who want a review on kanban basics. If your kanban basics are solid, then skip to Section 2.2 where we dive into how to expose time thieves and optimize your workflow using a Lean kanban flow approach.

All the examples may not apply to your specific situation. Think of this as a Lean kanban flow buffet. Take and implement what does apply to you, and use the rest to gain understanding of what people in other parts of the organization or in other companies might be dealing with.

Be forewarned—the outcomes of implementing these methods will depend on the investment level of participants from all parts of the organization. An investment made in mastering the practices in this book will position you well for seeing your work flow faster, which in turn will lead to the satisfaction that comes from delivering value sooner rather than later, from being more predictable rather than unreliable, and from making the work environment an all-around joyful spot rather than a troubled one.

Let's get started.

Learning is not compulsory...neither is survival.
—W. Edwards Deming

2.1

MAKE WORK VISIBLE

Take a look at Figure 4, an illustration by Philippe Kruchten.[1] (I've modified it to be hand drawn and I've used different colors.) It's a superb visual for highlighting important differences between visible and invisible work. A quick glance at this visual returns a meaningful message. Like a visual language, we see the relationship between invisible and visible work with respect to both negative and positive value. Highlighted in blue, "Architecture" radiates positive value. Unless it's an old, customized, fragile JDE implementation, wherein it would fall into the yellow technical debt area.

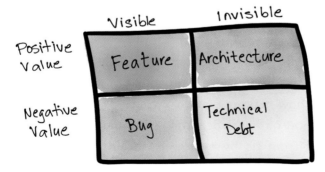

Figure 4. Visibility Grid

The image is a superb example of good visualization. It displays the four elements necessary to make a visual work: structure, usefulness, relevance, and honesty. This is what we want to accomplish when we make our work visible: easy on the eyes, accurate, meaningful, and efficient at a glance.

Once we have visibility of our work, we have the tools to manage the problems that slow our workflow down and are able to create the solutions for the unexpected when it arrives.

Another thing to consider when looking at the impact of relaying information visually is that two-thirds of the population are visual-spatial learners. Visibility matters when a majority of people think in pictures rather than in words. It's also important to know that this isn't a learned preference, visual-spatial learners have a different brain organization than auditory-sequential learners. They learn better by seeing than by hearing.[2] What does this mean? It means that it's a struggle for potentially two-thirds of your team when they can't *see* the flow and priority of the work they are doing. Making work visible allows your team to level up because it works *with* how their brains work instead of *against* it.

This section is a starting point for making your and your team's work visible. I'll be discussing different aspects of creating a kanban board as well as different ideas and concepts that help in understanding why they are important in the larger context of your work. The goal here is to show how making our work visible is an extraordinarily simple way to show our work demand—the amount and the type of work requested from us by everyone, including ourselves—and begin fixing the time-thief problem. You just have to jump in and start doing it to reap the benefits.

And kanban boards are all about jumping in because they start with an amazingly simple core—the To Do, Doing, Done design (Figure 5). The genius of this board design is that it's self-explanatory— you need to start working on something (to do), are working on something (doing), or are finished with working on something (done). Creating this straightforward kind of board is easy for any-one to do. You can apply it to all your tasks (your demand).

It also organizes your workload that may have otherwise been hard to see, or outright invisible, in a single view. Imagine this board hanging in your office: It's so simple and simultaneously so informa-tive that you don't have to explain it to others—anyone walking into your office will be able to look at the board and know what you're are working on and understand the state that the work is in, all without interrupting you with questions. Talk about a fast meeting.

Here is an example of one of our self-explanatory boards.

Figure 5. The To Do, Doing, Done Board

Most boards are, at minimum, made up of To Do, Doing, and Done columns (or equivalent names) that represent the state that the work is in. The work is represented by the work item cards. In Figure 5, the blue squares represent work item cards.

So, how does this kind of kanban board act in real-world action at your work?

First, there are some things to take into consideration. For instance, if you have a to-do list that looks like it's the size of *War & Peace*, then you may be asking if you really need to put *everything* on your board? No, you do not. The question becomes, what do you trim? Some things are so low on the priority list that it doesn't make sense to clutter your To Do column with them because that will distract you from the most important work. Also, by the time you finish your top three to five priority items, your next set of priorities will probably have changed.

So, what to-dos are okay to leave off the board? What provides the right amount of visibility for the team and the right amount of transparency for the rest of the organization? The answer is: it depends. What you make visible depends on what you do and what causes your team the most pain. Another consideration is the importance on making visible the uncertainties impacting your team and your company's business values. We'll tackle uncertainties and business values in Part 3, so let's focus on identifying what you do and what causes your team pain.

The guidance here for what to put on your board is to weigh the time cost of managing work items with the value received. It's not uncommon to see teams implement a policy whereby they don't create cards for work that takes less than fifteen minutes. Usually there are exceptions to this rule. Knowing when to break the rules is something that comes with experience.

My take on when to break the rules is when risk or uncertainty is high. Just because a task only takes ten minutes doesn't mean it's not important. Here are some guidelines. A ten-minute task probably doesn't need to be tracked unless one of the following is true:

1. **Only one person knows how to do it (Thief Unknown Dependencies).** Making the work visible can prompt some much needed cross-training.

2. **The work impacts other teams (Thief Unknown Dependencies).** As discussed in Part 1, cross-team dependencies can be very expensive. The one to two minutes it takes to create a card on a board is low enough overhead to be worth cross-team communication.

3. **Someone's job primarily involves doing tasks that last fifteen minutes or less, meaning if that person's work isn't tracked, then it's invisible (Thief Too Much WIP).** If a lot of the work is invisible, then it's awfully easy to pile too much WIP on top of that person's normal workload.

When you think about how to apply this guidance for what should *not* go on your board and when to make exceptions, you need to start asking questions about your demand, if you haven't already. Such as, what kind of work do you do? What kind of requests float across your desk, inbox, and chat window? What are the priorities of the work items on your list? In other words, what is the nature of your work demand? The answers will vary from team to team; different teams will have different demand. Here are examples of some of the stuff different teams do.

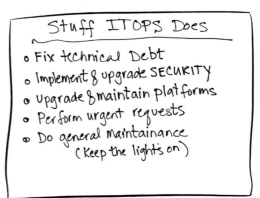

Stuff ITOPS Does
- Fix technical Debt
- Implement & upgrade SECURITY
- Upgrade & maintain platforms
- Perform urgent requests
- Do general maintainance (Keep the lights on)

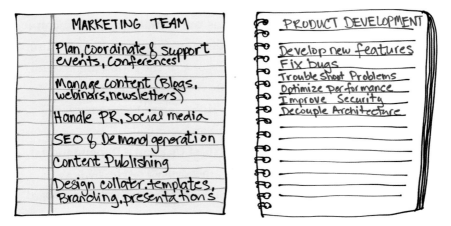

MARKETING TEAM	PRODUCT DEVELOPMENT
Plan, coordinate & support events, conferences	Develop new features
Manage content (Blogs, webinars, newsletters)	Fix bugs
Handle PR, social media	Troubleshoot Problems
SEO & Demand generation	Optimize performance
Content Publishing	Improve Security
Design collater. templates, Branding, presentations	Decouple Architecture

Each team has a different set of things they do, although sometimes they overlap. The Product Development team helps the IT Operations team troubleshoot security issues. The Marketing team helps test new features that the Product Development team delivers. Visibility across departments is something we'll get to in Section 2.3, when we cover the topic of dependencies.

In the early days at Corbis, before we made our work visible, I experienced endless amounts of heroics on holidays, weekends, at 3:00 a.m. I always had a list in my head of all the things outside of my control that constrained my efforts—a request from out of nowhere; a two-hour-long impromptu, unproductive meeting; a new project dropped on the team while we were still finishing up an older project...you get the idea.

I ranted (mostly to myself) as I worked furiously to finish the jobs on my plate about not having enough time in the day to fit all the demand in.

I'm here to say that unnecessary, overnight heroics suck. Here's the thing: Everyone I worked with at that time was doing the same thing.

We were all overburdened with too much WIP, conflicting priorities, and a disjointed work flow, resulting in negative impacts to our health as well as to the company's organizational health.

Looking back, I cringe at all that wasted time and how easily it would have been to alleviate the mutual pain if we had had visibility on all the work and its impacts to all the teams. But we didn't, so our time continued to be siphoned away by invisible demand. This is why it is so important to identify what prevents you and your team from getting work done. What randomizes your day? What causes your team pain?

Identifying team pain is a portion of the Demand Analysis exercise at the end of this section. It's satisfying and valuable because it gives permission for people to speak their minds instead of the typical restrained work language. (While ranting, just be mindful of the Lean pillar of respect for people.)

These are some examples of team pain:

TEAM PAIN

- Too many interruptions – can't focus
- Conflicting priorities – everything is a Priority one !
- Too many meetings
- No time for internal process improvements
- Too many different tools!
- Every reorg brings another process method.

– Burnout

Here are the top pain points that appear again and again in my Demand Analysis workshops (Thief Conflicting Priorities, at your service):

- **Too many interruptions**—I can't get work done.
- **Conflicting priorities**—everything is priority a one.

If these are two of your team's primary pain points, you are not alone.

One of the other lessons I took away from my time at Corbis is the need to consider other teams' pain carefully, particularly customer pain (or business pain). By this I mean your internal customers who are unhappy about the way your work results are impacting them.

It's important to make internal customer pain visible for a couple of reasons:

1. You are going to need your internal customers buy-in to limit WIP. Ignoring WIP limits allows the continuation of more demand than the team can handle. The cycle of being overloaded will continue and you won't realize the benefits of flow. Unhappy people are less likely to participate in solutions. Getting buy-in to limit WIP is easier when you ease customer pain along with easing your own team pain.

2. It's not just all about us. We must consider the whole system by using a Systems Thinking approach to optimize workflow across all teams in order to deliver business value. Optimizing in favor of one team can reduce the overall performance of the company. Organizational health includes discovering what our customers are unhappy about.

Once work demand and pain points are identified, you'll want to consider your work item categories. Creating categories for your work allows you to see different types of work—not all work is the same! It's important to have this clearly articulated because

BUSINESS PAIN

- Things take too long
- No visibility
- Unpredictable work
- Unaware of problems until its too late
- Simple requests get so complicated

different types of work may have different levels of urgency and different workflows need different rules to accommodate them. When we create categories for our work, we can collect the data necessary to create the metrics for the different types of work that shows us (and leadership) the health of our system.

Your work item type categories can be based on where requests originate from or who requests the work. Alternatively, they can be based on how the work is prioritized or the states that your work flows through. Since there are numerous ways to categorize your work item types, it's important to always consider what should be visualized in order to gather the proper data and to bring visibility to address problems.

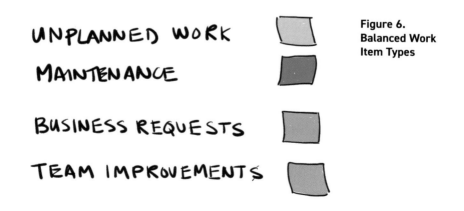

UNPLANNED WORK

MAINTENANCE

BUSINESS REQUESTS

TEAM IMPROVEMENTS

**Figure 6.
Balanced Work
Item Types**

Sometimes, the boss or just a few people determine the whole team's work item categories. This is something to avoid. The people doing the work should *always* be involved with designing their workflow management system for two reasons:

1. It helps ensure you have the right number and types of categories that cover the needs and demand of your entire team.
2. When people participate in creating something, they have ownership, which motivates them to invest in solving problems and achieving desired outcomes.

When deciding the number of categories, I've found that somewhere between three and seven is good. Any more than that and it becomes hard to manage, because for each category, you may have different rules, different metrics, and potentially different workflows.

The important thing to call out is that the Ops team in this example based their categories on their demand and the problems (team pain) they wanted to make visible. In this case, the volume of unplanned work and lack of capacity for making team improvements.

When you define your work item type categories, you are creating a legend to help your team work with a kanban board effectively. It also allows others, from management to other teams, to interpret the board when they see it.

Once you list the work your team does, determine your team and business pain points, and create your work item categories, you can start filling in some more detailed aspects of your work to further develop your team's visibility.

This detailed information will go in the fields of a work item. Again, involve the people who do the work for agreement on what data should take up space on the card. The information on the card should answer these questions: "What data do you need to manage workflow?" And "What do you want to measure?"

Here's a sample list that is in no way exhaustive but should get you up and running:

- Card ID
- Header
- Title
- Description
- Assignee(s)
- Comment section

- Tags for query capability
- Icons for extra visibility
- Priority
- Subtasks or connected card fields
- Date field for date driven requests

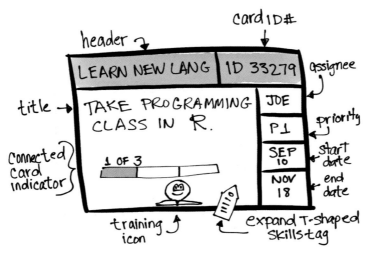

Figure 7. Work Item Type Example

Once you have your work item card designed, your team can immediately create cards for the work they are currently doing and pop these cards on your board. At a single glance, you've got a pretty good view of what your team is working on. Figure 8 is from an IT Operations team who categorized their work based on the combined desire to balance internal requests (team improvements) and business requests, and the need to support both unplanned work and regularly scheduled maintenance. On this board, the team just finished an expedited request (yellow), and they're currently working on one business request (blue) and one maintenance item (green). Next up in the To Do column is a team improvement item and a business request (orange) (blue).

Figure 8. To Do, Doing, Done Board with Colors

Often, teams need more granularity within the Doing column. It's common to see a Doing column split out further to represent some kind of feedback, test, or validation work before the work moves to Done, as seen in Figure 9. Initially, there is a degree of reader involvement necessary to render board transitions meaningful, but after several views it becomes obvious that cards are now in a different state: The business request is now in review, and the maintenance work is still being implemented.

Things really start to become visible when you have a To Do, Doing, Done board with some work items on it (as seen in Figure 10). It

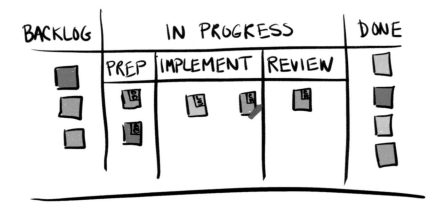

Figure 9. Expanded Doing Column

becomes even more helpful when you've thought on those pain points you and your team have listed and vote on the top two or three that you want to make visible. If it's a pain point, making it visible makes it easier for you to do something about it. I've found that it just takes an engaged group of dedicated team members to bring extra, much needed visibility to those items that are pain points for your team.

As you do all this, keep in mind that there is no sense in over engineering a kanban board design up front. Keep it simple. If extra granularity is needed, it will become self-evident through usage. Once you have your current work visible on the board, it's going to change after you take it for a test drive with your team. Avoid analysis paralysis at this point. It will take some time for your board design to stabilize (two or four or six weeks, depending on the maturity of the team).

In the meantime, head on over to Section 2.2 and go catch a thief.

Demand Analysis

PURPOSE: To identify the kind of work the team does and the related work problems (the team pain and business pain). These items will become inputs to the board design itself in later exercises.

🕐 *Time: 30 to 60 minutes*

MATERIALS:
- Markers
- Flip chart paper or a whiteboard

INSTRUCTIONS: List out the different types of work your team does. Refer to the IT Operations, Marketing, and Product Development team examples on pages 51 and 52 for ideas.

Then, list out any roadblocks preventing you and your team from finishing work. You can take a look at some examples of the team pain points on page 53.

When making your list, be specific. If your IT team's work is late because of constant interruptions due to competing priorities, note it. If your Marketing team's work is late because work piles up in the Design department, note it. This is your time to rant about the things you usually just mutter about. Come on, get it out.

Shining a light on these bottlenecks in your Lean kanban flow design will help make it possible for you to begin to fix the pain.

Next, list out your customer and/or business pain points. See page 55 for inspiration. Occasionally, someone in my workshops will tell me that their business executives are all really happy, and to that I want to call bullshit. No problem is a problem.

Identify Work Item Types/Categories

PURPOSE: To categorize the different kinds of work in order to support different workflows, different degrees of priorities, and applicable metrics.

🕐 *Time: 20 to 30 minutes*

MATERIALS:
- 3 x 3 multicolored stickies
- Markers/pens

INSTRUCTIONS: Here's where you and your team decide on what types of work to make visible via cards that will flow across your board. Anywhere from three to seven card types is reasonable. Each card is assigned a color. If your team struggles with wanting more card types, you can create a catch-all category for tasks that have the same workflow, and use tags and icons to differentiate them. Create a legend to refer back to.

Card Design

PURPOSE: To design useful, relevant, and good-looking work items that will provide people with the necessary information about the work.

🕐 *Time: 20 to 30 minutes*

MATERIALS:
- 3 x 3 stickies
- Markers/pens

INSTRUCTIONS: Identify the data that you want to capture on your cards and create fields for the data. If you're using an electronic tool, this part of the design will be done for you. If you're using a physical board, consider what fields you'll need to capture thievery problems.

Workflow Mapping

PURPOSE: To make work visible in order to see what is being worked on, what state the work is in, and the problems associated with potential disruptions and delays to the flow of business value.

🕐 *Time: 40 to 60 minutes*

MATERIALS:

- Flip chart or whiteboard
- 3x3 multicolored stickies
- Markers/pens

INSTRUCTIONS: First, ask yourself what pain points or hidden information you want to make visible. This is the fun part. Grab your team and, using a big whiteboard or flip chart (if you don't have a whiteboard or flip chart, use stickies on a wall or window), begin with three columns: Options (Backlog), Doing, and Done. Make the Doing column wide so you can break it up into more columns if need be. Place your existing work on the board and discuss what work states you'll want to have visibility on.

Now, let's have a look at how to make the time thieves visible so we can do something about them.

1. List the different types of work you do (demand and where it comes from).
2. Group the items into overall categories of work.
3. Discuss which work type seems to cause the biggest problem. Why is it a source of issues?

This will be your working kanban board to use throughout Part 2 of this book.

KEY TAKEAWAYS

- Visual-spatial learners think in pictures rather than in words. They have a different brain organization than auditory-sequential learners. They learn better by seeing than by hearing. Remember—two-thirds of the population are visual-spatial learners.

- Making work visible is one of the most fundamental things we can do to improve our work because the human brain is designed to find meaningful patterns and structures in what is perceived through vision.

- Visuals can show business pain points and other hidden information.

- We can use visual systems like kanban boards to help make work visible.

Multitasking is merely the opportunity to screw up more than one thing at a time. —Steve Uzzell

2.2

AMBUSH THE RINGLEADER

Back porch office, 8:35 a.m.

Deep into a metrics review focused on the evaluation of median cycle time, my eye perceives a tiny alert in the top right-hand corner of my screen. Before it flashes away, I see a blurb from Liz that asks, "Hey, do you have five minutes?" So, what do I do? I respond to Liz and say yes because I adore her. We do things for people we like— it's one of the five reasons we take on more work than we have capacity to do. And with that short exchange, I've added more work to my already full day.

As mentioned in Part 1, understanding and being aware of these five reasons is golden. The first reason is pretty basic: as team players, we don't want to let our tribe down, and as mentioned before, we get endorphins from saying yes.[1] The second reason is fear of public humiliation or of getting fired. The third is that we do stuff for people we like. The fourth reason relates to the fact that people are optimistic creatures, which leads us to think we can finish tasks faster than we actually do. Of course, things almost always take longer than we think they will. And finally, the fifth reason is that starting something new and shiny is more fun than doing the grunt work it takes to finish something old and unglamorous.

All five reasons are a part of Thief Too Much WIP's toolkit. As we have discussed previously, Thief Too Much WIP is the ringleader of all the other thieves. While it is bad enough on its own, Thief Too Much WIP infiltrates all the other time thieves and exacerbates the problems that are created by dependencies, unplanned work, conflicting priorities, and neglected work.

Let's take a look at a quick refresher on WIP. Remember, too much WIP means that work arrives faster than you can complete it. It's all the work you've started but not yet finished—all the partially completed work. Because Thief Too Much WIP scatters our attention across multiple things, it steals our time, our money, and our ability to deliver high quality work. This results in others having to wait longer than they'd like to get what they want, and you losing money due to the delay. Thief Too Much WIP steals time away from getting things done sooner rather than later. And because we cram to finish, the result is not the beautiful, masterly crafted product we want.

You know you have too much WIP when:
- Context switching is common.
- New tasks are started before older tasks are finished. In other words, we say, "Yes, I'll do that," even though we haven't finished a bunch of other stuff that is already on our plate.
- Work gets neglected and ages.

When you find yourself frequently context switching or when you get asked that five-word question, "Do you have five minutes?" and you say yes, you allow yourself to be yanked out of the flow zone and into the detour zone.

But there's hope! Tracking WIP can help you avoid further distraction and prevent Thief Too Much WIP from stealing your evenings and weekends.

There are many ways to track WIP. The following example (Figure 10) helps expose WIP and starts by dividing WIP into three major categories based on who requested the work:

- *Silver bullets* are urgent requests to do something right away, usually initiated by someone in a leadership position. They are in a category of their own because of their urgent priority (perceived or otherwise).
- Business requests, including feature work, content, and design, are the things IT does that "the business" promotes, manages, tracks, and is heavily involved with.
- Teamwork is the stuff IT does that teams initiate, such as dealing with bugs, technical debt, security, platform upgrades, and maintenance.

Again, this is just one way to categorize work; there are other ways that we'll explore a bit later.

Breaking work down into categories helps people better visualize the flow of work, which in turn aids them in understanding the communication needs of their team and of people outside the team. Recognizing and addressing these needs within the team is relatively easy. Outside the team, this task is harder, usually because extra effort is required to ensure the right person gets the right information. And silver bullets probably require special communication with the boss, because it was likely the boss's boss, if not the VP (or someone higher up the food chain), who made the initial silver bullet request. If not them, then someone they listen to and/or whose opinions they take seriously. (We do stuff for leadership to reduce fear of public humiliation or of getting canned.)

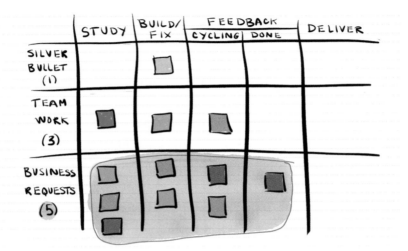

Figure 10. Expose WIP

Horizontal swimlanes are sometimes added to kanban boards for extra visibility or as a way to set up WIP limits. Swimlanes are lanes dedicated for a particular kind of work to flow through. A common swimlane seen at the top of many boards is a lane for *expedites* (work items that have some urgency around them and need to be expedited).

WIP limits are often set at the top of the columns of a kanban board to keep the linear flow of work in check, but they don't have to be. How you impose WIP limits is up to you *and* your team, those folks who are impacted by the work. There are several ways to set WIP limits. WIP limits per work item type, per swimlane, or per column are common options.

WIP limits per person are sometimes the first step folks new to kanban take in order to stem the bleeding of overburdened people. More advanced teams set WIP limits at team levels in order to optimize workflow at the bigger-picture level, instead of just the local level. This helps multiple teams to collaborate on team goals instead of focusing narrowly on individual goals.

Visuals like this help team members hold each other accountable with transparency. The WIP limits add tension to the system. People are compelled to innovate and resolve issues preventing them from finishing their work. WIP limits provoke necessary conversations. Some may start uncomfortably, but again, the tension from WIP limits inspires teams to get creative and prevail. WIP limits protect people from having to play catch up, and they impose rules that help you get stuff done. It's the WIP limits that create the necessary tension in the system. They give permission for people to say, "No, I can't take that on right now; my plate is full." They are the constraint that enables the completion of work.

A simple three swimlane board (such as in Figure 10) gives each swimlane its own WIP limit.

Silver bullet requests tend to come directly from leadership. This swimlane is sometimes called the VP lane. CIOs and VPs often don't realize the disruption created when they ask for things outside of the standard process. Bringing visibility to silver bullets helps show the cost associated with these requests. All work, including invisible WIP, has an associated cost, so make it visible! Silver bullets may well be worth the cost, so to these we say, "We know this is important, and we'll do it, but you only get one of these at a time." Limiting silver bullets to one at a time is just one example.

Teamwork in this visual consists of what I call revenue protection work; namely, fixing technical debt and security work.

Business requests are revenue-generating work. This swimlane is shaded pink in the figure because they've gone over the WIP limit of five, which prompts people to take a step back and ask, "What's going on?" It's helpful when others keep us honest. It's a bit like being on a diet—it's easier to avoid sugar when people are there to watch you order dessert every time you go out.

Remember, categorizing work by who requested it brings visibility to the communication involved—internal, external, or leadership.

Notice that the items in the feedback column in Figure 10 are not delivered yet and will now take longer to do. Flow requires clear and prompt feedback. Waiting on feedback from others is one of the biggest delays in workflow. The longer it takes to get feedback, the easier it is to forget details and the harder it is to be able to pick the work back up again. Like rotten fruit, knowledge decays faster than we'd like. Prompt feedback helps us negotiate challenging demands and adjust our tactics to maintain the flow state. It also encourages us to finish work already in progress before launching into shiny new work, no matter how much it glitters. Visualizing work through the lens of flow improves team communication and understanding.

Speaking of visualizing work, I am reminded of the visual language that occurs with kanban board designs. The "pictures" on the board (the board structure, card avatars, icons, and symbols) are easily received information. We need very little education to get the message. The writing on the board (the lane headers and on the cards) is perceived information. It can take some specialized knowledge to decode the abbreviated text and acronyms, but once they are known, a quick glance at the board returns volumes of information immediately. The combination of pictures and writing responds to our need for a nimble, unified language.

If you think about it, metered onramps are a combination of pictures and text. The traffic light is the picture, and the sign below it provides the text. A freeway onramp constrains traffic flow to allow for safer merging. The meter is only needed when there is high traffic. Have you ever tried to merge onto a freeway at rush hour when the metering lights aren't working? Yikes.

If you want to be more predictable, limit WIP to the team's capacity. What is the team's capacity, you ask? Good question. Don't let it be 90–100%. We'll cover why in Part 3.

Keep in mind that it's okay to start with a simple approach to limiting WIP. Taking small steps toward a goal is something Lean coaches counsel people to do all the time. You've got to start somewhere. Starting with a thin layer of something good is sometimes the only way to get started. Sometimes trying to make too big a change to your current process, such as implementing a strict set of WIP limits, could cause you to crash and burn. No one wants that to happen.

Limiting WIP also has the advantage of limiting interruptions. I have a tiny wood stove, which comes in handy when the power goes out. To conserve energy, I used to use it every day during the winter, regardless of the power being out or not. Unfortunately, the overhead for stoking and attending a small wood stove every thirty to forty-five minutes is high due to the interruption of work. But, if the fire lasted ninety to one hundred twenty minutes, I'd be fine with it because ninety to one hundred twenty minutes allows me time to concentrate long enough to make progress on complicated work.

When juggling five balls in the air, the amount of attention given to each ball is but a fraction of a second. There is an almost continuous need to switch your focus to the next ball. The same is true when handling five different work items. You can only give each one so much attention before you are interrupted by one of the other items. The more WIP, the more interruptions. It's easier to juggle three balls than five balls, and in the business world, it's easier to finish something and get it delivered and off your plate when there are fewer things to focus on.

Explore the Five Reasons Why We Take on More WIP

PURPOSE: To acknowledge that many (if not most) people take on more work than they have the capacity for, to hear and empathize with team members on why it happens, and to discuss *countermeasures* (actions taken to counteract problems) for how to deal with this common phenomenon.

🕐 *Time: 15 to 30 minutes*

MATERIALS:
- One pen per person
- Several 3 x 3 inch sticky notes per person
- Stopwatch

INSTRUCTIONS: Participants begin by pairing off with their neighbors and asking each other this question: "Why do you take on more work than you have the capacity to do?"

Allow two to three minutes for the interviewee to respond, while the interviewer jots down one answer per sticky note. Then switch roles.

Once everyone is done, have a group discussion about the reasons people offered. Then, discuss ideas for how to deal with people's desire to say yes when they don't have enough capacity. Be sure to specifically explore what to do when the request comes from someone they like or from a boss.

Variation 1: Ask each person to write their own answers on sticky notes if networking is unnecessary, such as with a group of people who already know each other.

Variation 2: Ask the group to collectively group similar responses together and post them on a wall to bring visibility to the most common responses.

KEY TAKEAWAYS

- Thief Too Much WIP infiltrates all the other time thieves, upping their damage and making them all the more difficult to control.

- There are many ways to set WIP limits. WIP limits per column, per work-item type, or per swimlane are common options.

- WIP limits create the necessary tension in the system. They are the constraint that enables people to complete work.

- Invisible WIP has a cost, so make it visible!

- Categorizing work by who requested it is just one approach to visualizing work. It's one that brings visibility to the communication involved— internal, external, or leadership.

- Visualizing work through the lens of flow improves team communication and understanding.

- The combination of pictures and writing meets our desire for a unified language. Use this combo to your advantage.

The hardest thing we do is communicate across teams.
—Troy Magennis

2.3

EXPOSE DEPENDENCIES

San Francisco, 2012

A large organization launches their third Agile transformation. A new team of consultants arrives to assess the situation. The new Agile teams are organized into subteams of five to nine people. Pizza is frequently delivered to these teams. (Remember the pizza problem from Section 1.2?) They had heard about the success Google had with two-pizza teams, and so this large organization decided it would work for them too. Many stories impacted other teams. They called these stories "away" stories because you had to go away to another team to solve the problem. Away stories impacted approximately 92% of the teams. Lots of people seemed to be away, well, a lot.

Thief Invisible Dependencies (aka Thief Unknown Dependencies) sneaks up on teams. A stealth-like time thief, Thief Unknown Dependencies reminds me of something someone once said to me that stuck: "By the time you find out you suck, you have sucked for a very long time." Similarly, by the time invisible dependencies are reported, you are already in deep water. The damage is done. But have heart—There is, as always, hope. This thief tends to thrive, predictably, when many teams work on different parts of one big system. The more teams, the higher the probability that more features are worked on at the same time, and this opens the door for more dependencies.

You know Thief Unknown Dependencies is robbing you when you hear, "Oh, by the way, so and so made this change/did this thing," and your jaw drops. Or worse, you get blindsided by the arrival of an unexpected instant messages from another team indicating a devastating problem. The hardest thing we do is communicate across teams. So, what do you do now? All the pizza in the world can't placate Thief Unknown Dependencies.

When a crisis occurs with one project team, people from other projects can be pulled off of their work to address the crisis. This leads to what is known as a high coordination cost. When the coordination cost between teams is high, people aren't available when you need them to be—and a project manager is often put in place to coordinate.

A large organization on their third Agile transformation attempted to deal with coordination issues by using spreadsheets. Dependency spreadsheets began floating around between some of the teams. This meant that some teams were in the know and some teams were blind to it. The hardest hit teams were shared services teams that supported multiple departments.

The consultants decided to try and minimize this risk. After some thinking, they came up with the following ideas to bring visibility to and deal with the dependencies:
1. Use cross-functional team stand-ups to flag dependencies.
2. Identify dependencies using a dependency matrix.

3. Implement explicit rules for work flowing between different team kanban boards.

4. Create a rotating dependency scout role—an enterprise-wide system architect who knows the system inside and out.

The idea of using cross-functional team stand-ups to flag dependencies was quickly abandoned because it was impractical, if not impossible, for groups of impacted people to attend numerous daily team stand-ups. The coordination cost was too high, and it would result in people spending all day in meetings.

The dependency matrix idea, however, had some real merit. One clever consultant created a floor-to-ceiling dependency matrix, which looked sort of like Figure 11 but much bigger:

Figure 11. Physical Dependency Matrix

INCOMING DEPENDENCIES	form button	tabbed panel	Param	Remote call UI	Component-fly	Restful action	Action Mapper	filter dispatcher	Servlet dispatcher	Portlet URL Helper
form button										
tabbed panel	1									
Param	3	7								
Remote Call UI	6				8	2		6	9	
Component-fly			5	7			11		10	
Restful Action			3							
Action mapper		2								
filter dispatcher				10						4
Servlet dispatcher		5								
Portlet Url Helper					2					

Numbers in boxes refer to the number of times that the dependency occurs, from the component shown at the top to the component shown on the left.

With everything laid out like this, people could begin to see the problems that resulted from having so many dependencies. It took a long time to finish stories because the experts capable of solving the issues weren't available when needed.

When a bunch of two-pizza teams have a lot of dependencies between them, how much time is spent coordinating? It's true, we like small teams because they can move fast. Just realize that by moving fast as an individual team, you're less able to move fast at the organization level due to the high coordination impacts from having a large number of dependencies.

Now, what to do about dependencies? If they are a problem for you and your dependency matrix, or if software isn't providing the necessary visibility, then you must find a way to make them visible across impacted teams.

Snazzy electronic automatic dependency mappers exist, but not many teams seem to take advantage of them. If you've got one in place and it works well (your dependencies on specialists or tightly coupled architecture don't cause you grief), then that's great. It's still good to have a clear understanding of other ways to visually depict dependencies.

Sometimes, dependency mapping involves good, old-fashioned arts and crafts. Part of the joy of making work visible lies in tapping into those long-dormant, construction-paper-and-colored-markers skills from your elementary school days.

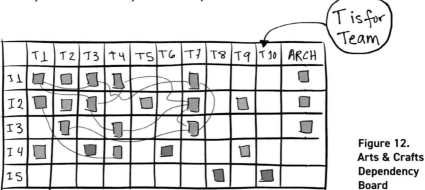

Figure 12.
Arts & Crafts
Dependency
Board

Note the last column on the board in Figure 12 titled "ARCH," which is short for architecture review. The intent of the architecture review is to provide expert guidance and support to enable the desired business functionality. It is not meant to be an authoritative approval moment.

If these options do not appeal to you or are not accessible to you, then take a look at Figure 13 which shows another way to visualize dependencies via your kanban board using a swimlane of its own.

Figure 13.
Dependency
Swimlane
Board

Design your board(s) to keep Thief Unknown Dependencies far away as shown in Figure 14.

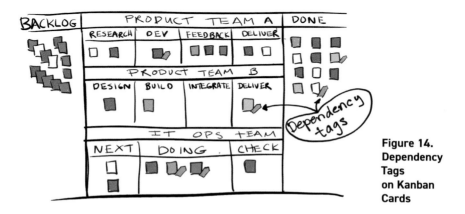

Figure 14.
Dependency
Tags
on Kanban
Cards

Or, visually call out dependencies between different teams so they can be broadcasted widely to reduce expensive business pain.

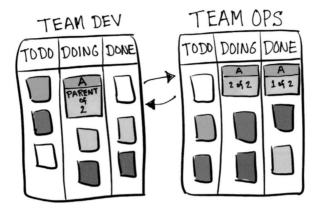

Figure 15. Show Dependencies Between Different Teams

Teams rarely work in isolation. If a skill set is needed from a different team, then hand-offs between the two teams need to happen. To avoid the "out of sight, out of mind" issue, visualize work flowing between teams. This helps people anticipate work that's headed their way and avoid "Oh, by the way, you need to do this thing today" situations. It also provides them with a heads-up on potential issues that are coming their way, which is usually much appreciated. Visualizing important cross-team information helps communicate across teams.

Small Agile teams are pervasive across the IT industry, and it makes sense. Nothing beats a talented, motivated, and cohesive team that makes fast decisions and can produce amazing results. In situations where the team has everything it needs to design, build, and deploy the product, then lucky you—Thief Unknown Dependencies is not stalking your neighborhood.

However, large organizations with many teams are not so lucky in this regard. At a certain point, the organization has grown to where it's impractical for lots and lots of people working on lots of different projects to be aware of every decision that impacts them (such as architecture changes and new third-party integrations). The more teams, the higher the probability that more dependencies are going to sneak into your day, project, objective, and so on. The more WIP, the greater the likelihood of Thief Unknown Dependencies hunting you down.

This is why you must expose dependencies—to avoid teams from unintentionally breaking existing functionality. Ask any team whose code has been broken by another team because they were unaware of a dependency created by that team—it's no fun troubleshooting a broken production environment while customers complain about your company on Twitter. Be informed and inform others, use whatever method works best in your situation, and remember that starting simple is better than not starting. Increased visibility helps get you to the next level. It may even help you to get leadership buy-in for organizing by product teams instead of by project teams—something to consider if your current organizational structure isn't serving you very well.

The problem is that project teams are short lived. Project people disband after dumping their project onto the Sustainment or Operations team and head off to work on another project. This transition is costly and time consuming. In the project team's rush to make project due dates, things get left out—you know, like dependency information. This introduces more WIP into the system because the team on the receiving side must interrupt the team on the delivery side to get the necessary information needed to run the new stuff.

In this way, the project team's expertise becomes a domain knowledge dependency. The WIP piles up because by the time Operations interrupts the people from the project team, the project team people are already off and running on something new, and now they need to context switch back and forth until the old project is stable or the new caretakers are effectively cross-trained, because, well, dependencies.

Organizing teams around a product allows the people who developed, tested, and delivered the functionality to stay in their area of expertise. There is no need for complex, dependency-driven handovers. Instead, organizing teams by product decreases dependencies during hand-off to ongoing operational support.

The project/product distinction is an important one for many reasons, so let's touch on that here for a moment so we don't conflate or confuse the two, especially since one is more productive than the other. Projects are delivered as one big monolithic thing, meaning that coordinating all the activities within a big release is difficult and slow. Projects create big batches of work that are handed off to others at the end of the project to deliver and maintain. Projects come and go and require extra coordination and communication to set up and organize temporary teams. Many issues can arise when maneuvering through a cumbersome, project-oriented process.

In contrast, organizing and managing by product keeps the same group of people with the necessary expert domain knowledge consistently involved. Those who develop the product features don't leave; they stick around to deliver changes to prod and maintenance. Project teams tend to be measured by vanity metrics (e.g., test teams within a project team are measured by the number of software bugs), whereas product teams are measured by the business value derived.

Senior Director of Technology at Pivotal Cornelia Davis noted in conversation at the 2017 DOES Forum, "Architecture is *so* tied to how we do our work. The preferred architecture is loosely coupled components, individual microservices, built by individual teams—autonomous product teams, not project teams."[1]

EXERCISE

The "Oh, By the Way" Dependency Matrix

PURPOSE: To bring visibility to dependencies across teams, to help people anticipate what's headed their way, and to prevent delays from unknown or invisible dependencies.

🕐 *Time: 60 to 90 minutes*
(possibly longer for very large teams)

MATERIALS:
- Large whiteboard or large paper or wall space
- Sticky notes
- Markers
- Pizza (absolutely essential)

INSTRUCTIONS: Gather up the detectives on your teams. Their mission, should they choose to accept it, is to investigate and visually capture dependencies across all teams that could negatively impact their work.

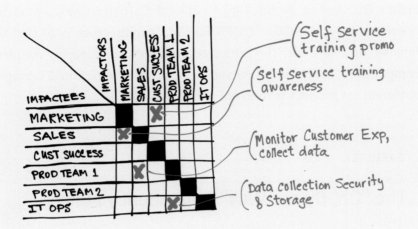

Figure 16. Exercise Example

Draw a large square graph with columns and rows. Using sticky notes, populate the column headers with your team names. Populate the row labels with the same team names.

The rows show teams that are impacted. The columns show teams that impact others (the impactors, if you will).

Identify the outputs from each team that create work for another team and write that number in the intersecting square.

For example, a customer success effort to provide self-service training content impacts Marketing and Sales because of the awareness required to promote and support presales. Sales requires monitoring of the customer experience and collecting customer data for personalized offers and promotions, which impacts Product Team 1 because of changes to the website and data collection. Product Team 1 in turn impacts IT Ops due to security and data storage requirements.

Your job here is to identify dependencies between teams for an important upcoming feature or project, and mark an X in the intersecting square where dependencies exist. Each cell of the matrix represents one or more dependencies between the two intersecting teams. Capture the dependencies themselves on the matrix.

Once your cross-team dependencies are identified in the matrix, discuss which actions can be taken to reduce the risk of breaking or negatively impacting another team's work.

Variation 1: Include upcoming risks in the matrix addition to dependencies.

Variation 2: Instead of teams, call out software components in the dependency matrix.

KEY TAKEAWAYS

- Small teams can move fast, but if there are dependencies between them, you pay the price of not being in a position to move fast as a whole organization.

- Design your board(s) to highlight dependencies to keep Thief Unknown Dependencies far away.

- Visually call out dependencies so they can be broadcasted widely to reduce expensive business pain.

- Visualize dependencies between different teams' kanban boards.

- Organize around product teams to reduce the problems associated with projects.

In these times I don't, in a manner of speaking, know what I want;
perhaps I don't want what I know and want what I don't know.
—Marsilio Ficino

2.4

THE PERFECT CRIME—
UNPLANNED WORK

Los Angeles, 2013

I asked two IT project managers responsible for supporting the team of forty-one engineers what prevented them from getting work done. Their immediate response was *constant interruptions*. They were being bombarded with project status questions from other teams and product owners. So, we conducted a one-week experiment to capture interruptions. Every time an interruption occurred, they wrote it down on a yellow sticky note and placed it in the top lane of a four-by-six-foot mobile board on wheels (Figure 17).

The yellow stickies flowed across the top swimlane. Green sticky notes recording internal team improvements and other work impacting the project mangers (represented by miscellaneous colored stickies) drifted across the middle swimlane. And in the bottom swimlane, multiple colors of stickies represented the different projects they managed. At the end of the week, we counted ninety-two yellow stickies. Ninety-two! Most came from walk-up traffic asking about project status. The project manager's primary internal customers, the product owners, were in the dark about the status and number of projects.

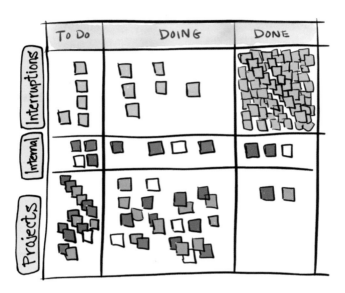

Figure 17.
A Study in
Interruptions

For the first time, the product owners could see the other projects competing with their own. And, importantly, they could understand why another project might be prioritized higher. They could also see for themselves the destructive nature of their interruptions. On the flip side, the project managers could see how little visibility the product owners had regarding the state of their project. The experiment also served as a chance to try out one board design before committing to a design using an electronic tool that is not be easy to change.

Visualizing interruptions is quite useful for exposing Thief Unplanned Work. Figure 18 shows another way to visualize interruptions. This team placed a pink dot on their work item every time that work was interrupted.

The pink dots gave them a quick way to visualize how interruptions impacted a strategy used elswhere is the grawlix string (#8%*@!) that shows the interruptions in an amusing manner.

Here's how it works. Each time work is interrupted, add one grawlix to the ticket on the board. The longer the grawlix series on the ticket, the longer the lead time and (presumably) the more irritated the engineer.

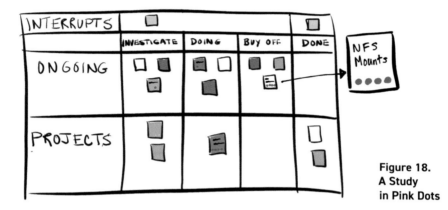

Figure 18.
A Study
in Pink Dots

It would be interesting to compare the grawlix count on work that is considered fun and engaging versus work that is not fun. I can imagine a ticket with work that no one wants to do (say a legacy system with a fun factor of zero or some tedious maintenance job) having an extremely long grawlix string.

Ours is a world filled with uncertainty, where everything is always changing. Sometimes we just don't know what we want or need until we see it. It's why there will always be unplanned work and why we need to plan for unplanned work. Because unplanned work can wipe out your objectives, unplanned work deserves visibility. All of us perceive a situation through the experience of our senses.

The board in Figure 19 exposes the experience of unplanned work visually. It's hard to repair invisible problems. Making work problems visible helps uncover the unknowns. Some of these may be scary to see, but once they're out in the open, the problems can begin to get fixed. As mentioned before, kanban may scare away the meek but is well suited for those with the courage to face issues, adapt to change, and fix problems.

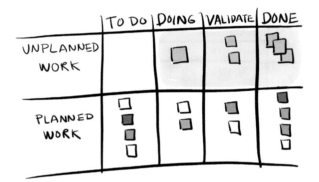

Figure 19. Expose Unplanned Work

Think of this board design as a way to visualize things that interrupt your week or ruin your day, things that take you away from delivering important business value because you are busy putting out fires. This unplanned work flows through its very own swimlane. A card is created for every piece of unplanned work.

There's usually resistance to this in the form of Platform Operations Manager Erik, who says, "I don't have time to create a ticket every time I get interrupted!" But after weeks of interruptions, the CIO wants to know why Azure isn't up and running in production. And what does Erik say? "We've been busy." This is the problem—there is no evidence of the issues preventing Erik from completing the platform work. It's a perfect crime. And Thief Unplanned Work goes home and collects $200 by passing go. When unplanned work is made visual, other people can see it and understand why work isn't done—and steps can be taken to prevent, or at least limit, unplanned work from taking over in the future.

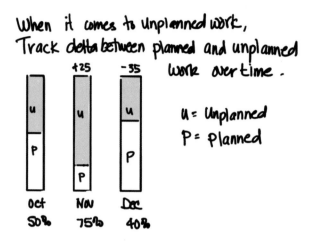

Figure 20. Monthly Delta Trend for Unplanned Work

Knowing the ratio of unplanned work to planned work helps when planning your workload capacity. Why? Because you'll have an idea of how to set WIP limits to accommodate important, unexpected, and urgent work. If every week there is 25–50% unplanned work, then allocate 25–50% of your WIP for potential unplanned work. Here's a way to do this:

1. Calculate your ratio of planned work versus unplanned work by dividing the number of unplanned work items completed last month by the total number of planned and unplanned work items completed last month. For example, if you completed 100 work items last month and forty of them were unplanned, the ratio is 40% unplanned work.

2. Given the above example, 40% of all your WIP should be reserved to handle unplanned work and low priority work. Low priority work is important work, just not the highest priority. This strategy provides you with capacity to handle unplanned work and/or to set the lower priority work aside in the event of a new critical request. It also helps you get important work done that might otherwise turn into an urgent critical request (as in, this server just reached max capacity) in the near future or further down the road. Either way, important work gets done.

3. Each month, view your ratio of planned work to unplanned work to see if the trend is moving up or down, and adjust your WIP allocation accordingly.

Note that we are talking about the amount of WIP here and not the amount of time. Allocating time is a different animal. Sometimes you hear managers tell people, "Allocate 50% of your time to do blah, blah, and set aside 25% of your time to do blah." But how do you really do that? You are a rare bird if you are fortunate enough to have a wide-open calendar which allows you to schedule half your day (say four hours) on blah, blah and a quarter of your day (say two hours) on blah. Because much of the day is likely sliced up with meetings, email, and context switching between tasks, getting two hours of uninterrupted time to work on anything can be a luxury.

You may be thinking that allocating your workload (your capacity) by WIP limits won't fly because your work items aren't all the same size. This is an area where size doesn't really matter because you can only work on so many things at a time. It doesn't matter how big or small something is when you can only truly focus on one thing at a time. It could be as small as a mouse or as big as an elephant (metaphorically speaking). When it's done, you move on to the next thing.

Interruption Busters

Try these strategies to create a consistent format for managing your time when tackling the challenge of making unplanned work visible:

- **The goalie:** Someone designated to run interference for the rest of the team. It is a rotating role, with the dual purposes of protecting others from interruptions and cross-training team members.
- **Office hours:** Just like with your teachers back in school, schedule a specific amount of time (a time-boxed amount of time) a couple of hours a week and let people know when they can get your time. Office hours give your colleagues a chance to drop in at *your* convenience.
- **Do not disturb hours:** A mirror image of office hours. Put a "Back in 1 hour" sign on your door or somewhere in your space to notify people when you'll be back. I block off 6:00 to 8:00 a.m. every day on my calendar. This is when I write and do yoga. My boss once asked me to attend a 6:30 a.m. meeting. I said no. I felt guilty doing that, but to get the important work done, we must ferociously protect time to do what matters most. And by saying

no, I established a precedent. No one expects me to be available for 6:30 a.m. meetings now.
- **Pomodoro:** A time management method using a timer to break down work into time-boxed intervals separated by short breaks.[1] Set a timer for twenty-five minutes and work on your task until the timer rings. When the timer rings, take a five-minute break. After four pomodoros, take a longer break (twenty to thirty minutes). Pomodoros give you permission to really focus. I used this method to finish writing this book.

These four strategies create consistency that help your team see when you're tackling your WIP.

During the 1960s, the coffee cart at HP rolled around at 10:15 every morning. All the engineers drank coffee and casually discussed top-of-mind issues. It was a goldmine condition that generated spontaneous collaborative advances. A lot of problems got unstuck at the coffee cart. In the 1970s, cost-cutting decisions were made to replace the coffee cart with a self-service coffee pot on the counter in the mini kitchen. Engineers still took a break to get coffee but not at the same time. No more set coffee break, no more spontaneous brainstorming. Gone were the unplanned collaborative developments— all in the name of cost savings. Some felt it was the beginning of the end for the great days of HP research and development.[2]

Just as regularly scheduled rendezvous (same place, same time) work as a catalyst for frequent dialogue on top-of-mind issues in need of discussion, consistency of work times and break times help establish habits to minimize interruptions. Consistency signals to people when they can have your attention and when they cannot. Consistency helps to minimize the damage from unplanned work.

The Interruption Reduction Experiment

PURPOSE: To reduce damage from interruptions using empirical evidence.

🕐 *Time: 45 to 60 minutes*

MATERIALS:
- Whiteboard
- Markers

INSTRUCTIONS: Gather the team to discuss ways to reduce the cost of interruptions. These might include having a goalie, scheduling office hours, scheduling do not disturb hours, and using pomodoros or a variant involving dedicated ninety-minute sessions. Which of these methods might apply to your team and why?

Come up with a hypothesis and experiment for a week. Regroup after the experiment to discuss your observations on the impact of the experiment on your team. What worked and why? What didn't work and why?

For example: Hypothesis—scheduling office hours will reduce interruptions. Schedule office hours from 1–2 p.m. on Monday, Wednesday, and Friday. Let everyone know you are available during these hours for impromptu questions. This signals people (creates a visual) when you are available and when you are closed for business.

KEY TAKEAWAYS

- There will always be unplanned work, therefore you should plan for unplanned work.

- Knowing the ratio of unplanned work to planned work helps you plan workload capacity.

- Size doesn't really matter when it comes to WIP limits—it doesn't matter how big or how small a chunk of work is when you truly focus on just one thing at a time.

- A consistent time and place for office hours and do not disturb hours helps to minimize the damage from unplanned work.

Many things may be important, but only one can be the most important. —Ross Garber

2.5

PRIORITIZE, PRIORITIZE, PRIORITIZE

Los Angeles, 2013

The six-by-four-foot mobile experiment board on wheels was positioned directly next to the project managers' desks and coincidently, but conveniently, positioned alongside the main footpath between the entrance to the engineering space and the kitchen. Everyone had to pass this board on their way to their desk in the morning and on their way out to lunch/coffee/home. It caught people's attention. Product owners studied it to see if they could find their projects on it. Scrum masters stared at it—unsure what it was all about. IT Ops Engineers darted glances at it with the uncomfortable familiarity and commiseration from being overwhelmed by massive interruptions that the interruption experiment exposed.

The visibility on interruptions was attention getting—and not just because it captured how often people were poking their heads into offices with unplanned requests but because it also showed the lacking prioritization policy.

Returning to interruptions, the opening experiment with the two IT project managers from the previous section—the one that captured interruptions—was deemed a success by the IT Ops Project Managers for several reasons:

1. It caught the attention of the VP of Operations, who used it to re-emphasize specific kinds of work that he wanted visibility on. These were requests related to capacity expansion, security, site reliability, and disaster recovery. These kinds of work items were flagged with symbols on the physical board and later found their way into the electronic version of the board.

2. It raised questions from product owners and other team members about the competing priorities of the thirty-three projects. Thirty-three projects! That's thirty-three projects in progress for a group of only forty-one people. Seems ridiculous doesn't it? But that's what happens when priorities are unclear—people take on more WIP.

Figure 21.
An Experiment
in Tagging
and Prioritizing

So, the experiment continued for a second week. This time, we cornered the lead engineer into stack ranking the thirty-three projects. He gave it his best shot. We were delighted to finally see that as he worked on it, we saw some prioritized order (Figure 21). But shortly after, the VP came by and disagreed with the priorities. This forced a necessary conversation, which was good, because the rationale behind how value was determined (at least from the VP's perspective) was now transparent.

This is the power of placing a four-by-six rolling visual along the main route for both the department entrance and the very important coffee room. It's unavoidable. The eye is drawn in and people stop to ponder. It provokes essential communication that would otherwise be conveniently dodged.

After that discussion happened, the projects were reprioritized based on the VP's input, a classic prioritization strategy known as *HiPPO* (highest paid person's opinion). And then an interesting thing happened. The next day, four new projects appeared, seemingly out of thin air, in the top right corner, all vying for the priority one slot. Thief Conflicting Priorities scored big that day, chuckling at the resulting drama created by inserting more chaos. (I wish we'd had a webcam aimed at that board; it would have been interesting to see how they got there.)

Beware the lack of good rules for prioritization—remember, when everything is a priority one, nothing is a priority one.

As always, it is possible to get out of this mess by employing the key concepts we've been building upon in this book—namely exposing time theft by making work visible.

For example, propose a prioritization strategy to kick off the conversation. You might use the A3 thinking process to do this. *A3* is a problem-solving approach using an international 11 x 17 inch (297 x 420 millimeters) piece of paper. (A3 gets its name from the size of paper of the same name). A3 encourages precise communication in an effective structure that cultivates understanding and agreement. One result of using A3 is that various options can be investigated and floated across the organization in a diplomatic fashion.

Because the A3 method helps you get understanding and agreement, it can be used to discuss prioritization methods. The goal with prioritization is to determine what to complete next in order to get maximum value in the shortest amount of time and to avoid multitasking due to competing priorities.

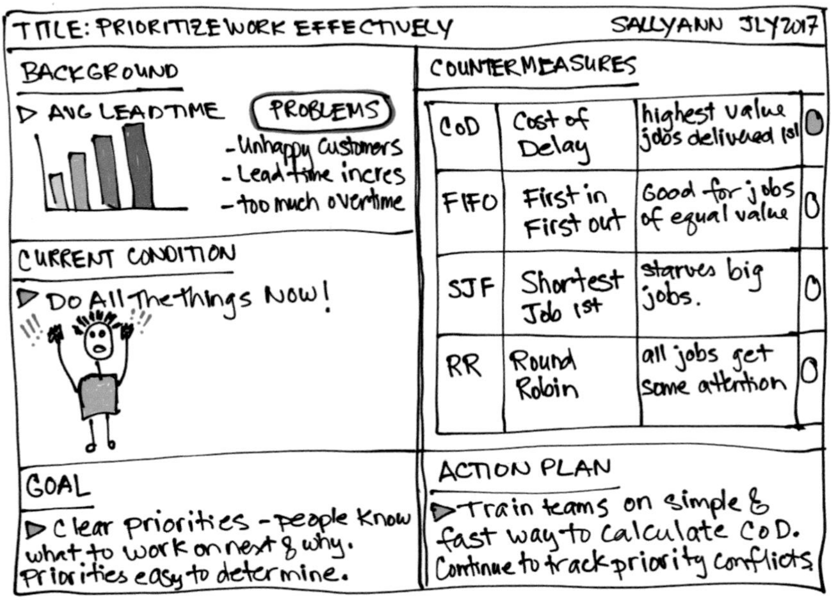

Figure 22. A3 Example

There are several ways to prioritize. Let's look at some of the more common methods:

- **Highest paid person's opinion (HiPPO):** Each job is assigned a priority by the most senior person in charge and processed accordingly. Remember the thirty-three projects prioritized by the VP?

- **Cost of delay (CoD):** A way of communicating value and urgency, CoD is a measure of the impact of time on the outcomes we want. This is an excellent approach for determining business risk, but difficult for many people to actually do.

- **First-in, first-out (FIFO):** *First-in, first-out* work is processed in a first-in, first-out fashion. It's a simple and fair process, such as at the movie theater, where the person ahead of you receives their movie ticket before you do.

- **Weighted shortest job first (WSJF):** *WSJF* gives preference to the shortest job with the highest CoD. WSJF is calculated by dividing the CoD by the job duration. The Scaled Agile Framework (SAFe) model uses a variant of WSJF, which attempts to include time critically.

There are many ways to prioritize work. The above list shows just some of the options.

Swinging back around to the LA IT Ops Engineering team that we opened the section with, notice how their prioritization approach evolved from, "Do all the things" to the lead engineer's opinion of what was a priority to the VP's or another executive's opinion of what was a priority—the HiPPO approach. If the VP or other executive has sufficient knowledge and experience, it is possible that their prioritization can be good enough. But problems occur due to their cognitive bias, misaligned goals, or overconfidence. We are often confident even when we are wrong,[1] and it can be hard for us to see when we are wrong. This is why making prioritization policies visible is vital—it drives the right conversations for delivering ideal outcomes.

In Part 1, clues were provided for detecting when Thief Conflicting Priorities is stealing your time. They include:
- Wasting time in meetings discussing priorities.
- Taking on new work because you are unsure what the priorities are.
- Being repeatedly asked, "When will my thing be done?"

Remember: Thief Conflicting Priorities is a close cousin of Thief Unplanned Work, which produces questions like:
- "When will my thing be done?"
- "This thing is a high priority!"
- "If we don't get _____ done by _____, we might all be looking for new jobs."

Here's one way to see the things that conflict with each other. Unplanned expedited work, project work, maintenance work—it's all competing with each other. When work goes on hold because someone says you need to do this other thing now, show that in your

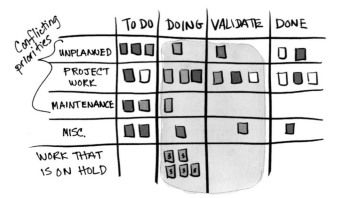

Figure 23. Exposing Conflicting Priorities

visibility efforts. Show that implementing the new security vulnerability fix got deprioritized because people had to do merit reviews. The idea is to make prioritization rules explicit. Otherwise, how are they made? By the loudest, most aggressive person? By the highest paid person?

Work takes a long time to complete because it sits in queues waiting for stuff to happen. It's not unusual for wait times to be more than 80% of the total time. Many organizations are blind to the queue problem. They tend to focus on *resource efficiency* instead of applying systems thinking to improve the efficiency of the whole system, end to end.

Cost of Delay (CoD)

Priority is only a problem when things aren't delivered in the desired timeframe. We know that trying to do everything at the same time increases the risk of delaying everything. And we know that choosing to work on one task puts other tasks on the back burner and

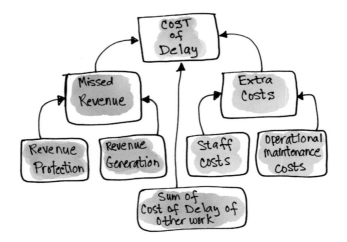

Figure 24. Inputs That Contribute to Cost of Delay

causing their delay. The goal, then, is to understand what work should be completed next in order to achieve the best possible outcomes. Quantifying the cost of the work that gets delayed is useful.

As mentioned in Section 1.1, cost of delay is a measure of the impact of time on the outcomes desired. CoD boils down to three things:

1. Reduced revenue or business value (CoD is not always about money)
2. Increased costs
3. The sum of the CoD of other work that is dependent on the work we are calculating CoD for

Let's take one of the thirty-three projects from the IT Ops Engineering team board, "Build out New Datacenter (BoNDC for short) to understand how the CoD could be calculated." Part of the Done criteria for Project BoNDC is for the old datacenter to close. Hence, the costs to keep the old datacenter running need to be included.

Old datacenter costs include floor space rental, power, heating and cooling, operating costs, and maintenance totaling $7,400/week.

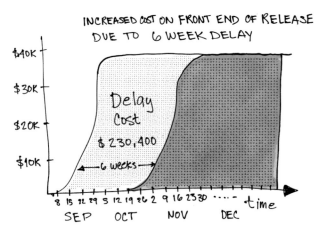

Figure 25. Cost of Delay

Additionally, a project manager spends 20% of their time managing the transition to the new datacenter: $400/week. Also included in the CoD is the CoD of Project P, which will improve performance but it is dependent on the completion of the new datacenter: 8 engineers (50%) × $2,800/week = $22,400/week. Furthermore, the cost savings from Project P (due to automation of manual processes) = $8,600/week.

The weekly CoD of BoNDC is $38,800/week. If BoNDC is delayed six weeks, the total CoD is $230,400.

CoD can be used to negotiate prioritization of work and to bring visibility to projects that have a bigger impact on the bottom line than the others. Visualizing CoD drives the right conversations and decisions around cost and revenue. As Joshua Arnold, thought leader and founder of Black Swan Farming, says,

> Cost of Delay combines urgency and value—two things that humans are not very good at distinguishing between.
> To make decisions, we need to understand not just how valuable something is, but how urgent it is.[2]

Hence, CoD communicates the impact that time has on value. Value usually means money, but not always. A non-profit health organization may consider value as the number of lives saved. Work then is prioritized based on the highest business value returned (economic or otherwise) rather than the theoretical ROI.

CoD considers all the impacts to what generates new revenue, what protects existing revenue, and all the expenses associated with running an organization.

Simply put, CoD has to do with two constantly changing variables: value and time. CoD asks the question, "What value is lost by the delay of something? How much will we lose if we deliver this thing twelve months later?"

The Line of Commitment

The line of commitment is a vertical line before a specific state that signals a commitment on your part to do the work. The tasks in the backlog are options, and they may never get done. But once work passes the line of commitment, it explicitly signals that it's been prioritized and is moving forward. It is no longer an option but a fully agreed upon and prioritized piece of work.

There is no second-guessing once work passes the line of commitment. The work will happen—and it will have a cost. How high the cost is depends on how long it's delayed due to the competition with other planned and committed work all vying for the same people's attention and resources.

**Figure 26.
Line of
Commitment**

Visualize Priorities

PURPOSE : To help you bring visibility to competing priorities and bring clarity to how work is prioritized. Most organizations have too many top priorities to achieve the level of focus they need in order to succeed.

🕐 *Time: 60 minutes*

MATERIALS:
- Your current workflow or kanban board

INSTRUCTIONS: Ensure those impacted have a voice in the discussion. Time-box each person's comments to no more than five minutes.

Questions to discuss:
- What is your prioritization policy and how is it visualized?
- How will you signal when work has been prioritized and is ready to be worked on? In other words—where is your line of commitment? How do people know which work to pull?
- How will you visually distinguish between higher and lower priority work?

- People take on more WIP when they are unclear on priorities. Establish an explicit prioritization policy to avoid too much WIP.

- The A3 problem-solving approach encourages precise communication in an effective structure that cultivates understanding and agreement. For more on A3, read *Managing to Learn* by John Shook.

- There are many ways to prioritize. Assigned priority, CoD, FIFO, HiPPO, and WSJF are some of these options.

- Visualize priorities so people are crystal clear on what constitutes the most important work.

- Think about the line of commitment. Bring clear visibility to work that is prioritized and fully committed but, if competing with other projects, will increase its cost of delay.

Never let something important become urgent.
—*Eliyahu Goldratt*

2.6

PREVENTING NEGLIGENCE

Small Town, USA, 2015

CTO Frank sighs heavily over his third Mountain Dew of the morning. It's the second time this week that the database server has hit maximum capacity utilization. The team can't get their heads above water long enough to perform seriously delinquent maintenance.

Like an old broken chair, it's easy to cast aside an aging request when a new request arrives in the backlog. But as we've discussed previously, the cost of starting new things before finishing old things is high. When too much work is in process, bad stuff happens: context switching increases, bottlenecks develop, dependencies rise, windows of opportunity close, and holidays arrive. And because things are delayed, people want to pile on more things—you know, "Let's add this other fix while the hood is up." This all causes work to take longer than it should and delays the delivery of business value.

An IT Operations team at one company I worked with had a work-flow where the last step before Done was Validate. There was no good process at the time to provide timely feedback, so work items just sat, waiting to be validated after they were delivered. The norm was to assume that all was okay if no one complained. While work sat idle in Validate, people pulled more work out of the backlog into "Implement." The Validate queue grew and grew until it had close to 100 work items. Many of the items delivered were indeed okay, but some were not, and those customers were unhappy.

When those downstream, internal customers mentioned that the work hadn't been delivered as expected, the IT Operations people took a long time to respond because they were already working on the next task. As the time grew between customer feedback and Operation's response, those customers became very unhappy and eventually gave up trying to communicate with Operations. They complained among themselves and to other departments. "Ops never responds," they said. "They're like a big black hole—hell will freeze over before they do anything," they groused. "What a worthless team." The Operations team's reputation slid down the drain.

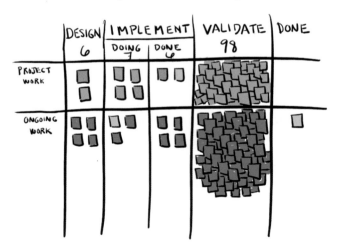

Figure 27.
The Validate Pit

The board in Figure 27 represents the IT Operations workflow. I show this board image in my workshop and ask folks, "Where is work stuck here?" It doesn't take more than a second before people respond with, "The Validate queue!"

This is the power of the unified language of kanban boards—the message is communicated instantaneously. Because the bottleneck lies in Validate, we must tackle the Validate queue first.

Here's the experiment we did: We set a timeframe to close the items sitting in the Validate queue. All items (called tickets by this group) that had not been updated in fourteen days or more would be closed. We asked a few key people what they thought, and we began to socialize the idea among the IT Operations and Development teams. No one really seemed too concerned by our proposal, so we prepared boilerplate comments to add to all the tickets sitting in Validate and communicated our plan across the Development and Operations teams. We told people that we were going to close the tickets on a set day and that they should let us know if they had any issue with it. That day, we closed 104 tickets, and only two people responded to say they still wanted to keep the ticket open. It felt so good to get all those tickets closed.

You may be thinking that the validate function was worthless if all those tickets could just be closed like that. Many of the tickets closed that day were ancient and already obsolete. Remember, other teams had given up on the Operations team and found other means to get the job done. But we didn't stop there.

The next part of the experiment included gradually reducing the number of days a ticket could sit idle (getting stale) in Validate. We gave the teams thirty days to adjust to idle tickets being automatically closed and then squeezed the timeframe from fourteen days to ten days for the next month. Teams adjusted and started validating tickets sooner. Unlike before, when the tickets were stale and all but forgotten, it was relatively easy for them to complete the validation because the work was still fresh in their minds.

This is one of the major problems with neglected work and an important reason why we should avoid it. Once the work has sat untouched for weeks or even months, we forget the details, and it takes a long time to dive back in. Thief Neglected Work loves it when work sits around so long that you no long remember what was happening. Smack Thief Neglected Work upside the head by keeping work clipping along at a smooth pace.

Of course, continuous improvement is always the goal, and thirty days later, we cut the timeframe from ten days to seven days. Thirty days after that, we went from seven days to five days. Why didn't we just start out with five days? Because five days never would have flown in the beginning. The change would have been too abrupt. Two weeks is, relatively speaking, a long time—it's not threatening to anyone. The gradual change allowed people to adjust and adapt. Because the Validate queue usually empties every five days now (sometimes things take longer, but now people update the ticket with comments keeping it active), the cycle time of the tickets has decreased dramatically. Work flows through the system quickly, and problems in Validate surface right away. With the Validate pit improved, we moved on to the next bottleneck.

Multitasking is an effective way to get less done. It's an effective way to give negligence free reign. When you try to do too many things at one time, you won't do any of them great, and sometimes you won't finish them at all. Neglected work is another term for partially completed work. Consider a partially completed bridge. It is already expensive, but it provides zero value until it's finished.

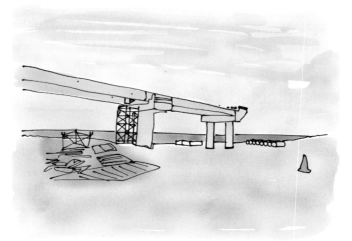

Thief Neglected Work steals time from you when important work becomes urgent. Good time-management means spending time on important things and not just urgent things. Make time to work on fire prevention so that you can reduce the amount of time you spend putting out fires.

Revenue-protecting work is a major target of Thief Neglected Work. Because the business is often unaware of what's involved in keeping a system secure, reliable, and functioning, revenue-generating work is considered a higher priority than intangible maintenance and sustainment work. In many companies, short-term revenue-generating work is top-of-mind for business people, but the long-term health of the platform system is rarely contemplated. As a result, revenue protection work takes a backseat until something blows up, such as a distributed denial-of-service attack or a corrupt finance database that brings down credit card fulfillment.

It's not intentional—people just tend to focus on doing their job and assume their coworkers will do the same and that everything will be fine. Humans are like that. We tend to avoid the annual doctor's exam until something is really wrong.

Call Out Neglected Work

Here's a way to make neglected work obvious. Flag work items that haven't moved or been updated within a certain number of days. In Figure 28 there are two flagged items, one for nine days and one for thirteen days, respectively.

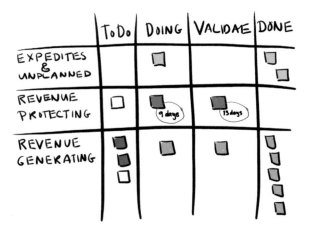

Figure 28. Expose Neglected Work

Then you can make aging work visible. Query all your WIP (so, not the backlog and not the done or archive work) in your system that hasn't been touched for thirty days. If that produces too many items to see at one time on the screen without scrolling, bump up the search criteria to sixty, ninety, or 120 days. I've seen teams with WIP over 300 days, so don't feel bad if you've got a few like that too.

To deal with those archaic items, schedule a ten-minute meeting (yes, just ten-minutes) every day directly following stand-up with the creator and the current assignee of the work.

Here's some language for you to use:

> **Subject:** Work Item # nnnnn (enter title of item here).
> **Invitees:** The creator of the work item and the current assignee of the work item.
> **Location:** Dominica's desk (or video chat if remote).
> **Description:** This work item is now famous. It's the oldest WIP in the system.
>
> Can we please take 10 minutes directly after stand-up tomorrow to see what it would take to close it?
>
> Many thanks!
> Dominica

These meetings should help you determine which projects are worth saving, which can be quickly wrapped up, and which are zombie projects that need to be purged. Remember, zombie projects are low-value projects that nevertheless consume time, energy, and money. Killing them helps reduce neglected work and allows you to deliver more important projects faster and with fewer interruptions.

Even though neglected work is not a priority, it still consumes some mental budget. Like that reminder on the fridge to schedule your annual physical, Thief Neglected Work stalks you every so often, distracting you just long enough to divert your attention away from what you should be focusing on. Here's what you need to do to get Thief Neglected Work off your back in three steps:

1. Acknowledge the neglected work sitting on your board that's not moving and the impact it has on other work.

2. To create space to finish the most important work, lower WIP to a discussion on priorities. Something has to give. Either give work the attention it needs, kill it, or move it back to the backlog.

3. Ruthlessly protect your time using some of the techniques mentioned in Section 2.4 and stop starting new work before finishing old work. As author Arne Roock says in his book *Stop Starting*, start finishing!

EXERCISE

Create an Aging Report

PURPOSE: To improve the flow of value by making stale work visible. An aging report shows WIP that is stale.

🕐 *Time: 40 to 60 minutes*

MATERIALS
- Large whiteboard or large paper or wall space
- Sticky notes
- Markers
- Computer (and, of course, a pizza)

INSTRUCTIONS: Query your work-tracking tool to find high-priority, yet partially completed work that has not moved or been updated in thirty days. If thirty days results in a huge list, then increase to sixty or ninety days. Randomly select seven to eleven of those high priority items. Statistically, seven to eleven is sufficient—as long as it's truly a random sample set.

For each of the seven to eleven items, note the following:

- The number of days the item has been stale (not been updated or moved or made any progress).
- The average cycle time for cards of a similar work item type.
- How many days the item has been in progress in comparison to other similar items.

Now, write down what happens if this item continues to be delayed for another week. Consider lowering your WIP limit and reprioritizing your WIP based on what might happen if the work is delayed. Identify the utmost valuable work currently on your board and separate out the lower value items. If possible, do an improvement blitz to push through the one highest priority item to get it delivered. Improve flow by making work visible. Remember the goal is to improve flow by making important, stale work visible.

KEY TAKEAWAYS

- Important work that is delayed becomes urgent, unplanned work.

- Visualize delays.

- Call out neglected work and purge low-value projects.

You don't learn to walk by following rules. You learn by doing and falling over. —Richard Branson

2.7

USEFUL BOARD DESIGN EXAMPLES

In this section, you will find examples of kanban board designs that are useful for making work visible in situations where time thieves cause particular damage. Think of this section as a kanban smorgasboard. Select what works for your context and pass by what doesn't.

Multilevel Board Design

In the same way that cross-team boards make hand-offs visible, multi-level kanban designs make multiple projects and cross-functional teamwork visible. A multilevel board design provides a big-picture view from the portfolio level to the team level, providing visibility of all the WIP. In Figure 29, high level programs one and two are connected to team boards where the work is performed. Teams break down their work into smaller batches and create work items.

If the work is handed off to another team, say from Development to Operations, then the parent work items are connected to cards on

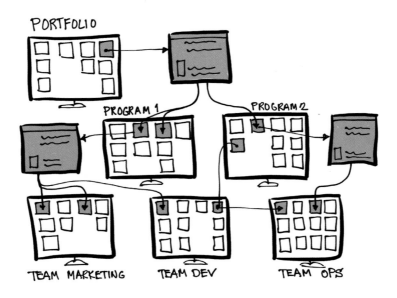

Figure 29. Multi-Level Board Design

the other team board. This signals hand-offs and makes work visible. It's not uncommon to see organizations with three levels of boards: a high-level board for the portfolio level, a mid-level board for different programs or *value streams*, and lower-level boards for team work.

Done vs. Done Done

It's the last step of the process and work is handed off to someone else to wrap up the loose ends. We can consider the work done—right? Not so fast. There's a chance that you might want to hold off on moving the work to Done in order to get visibility on work that isn't providing any value to the requestor yet.

Think of a box of cereal sitting on a grocery store shelf. Corn flakes don't provide any value to Kellogg's until a customer buys them. Like inventory sitting on a shelf, a newly developed feature or a bug fix doesn't provide much value to the requestor until they can get their hands on it.

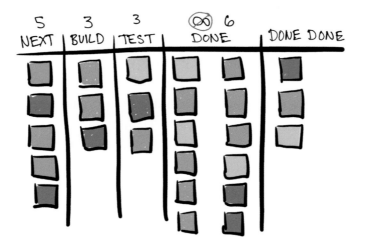

Figure 30. Done Vs. Done Done

This is where the Done Done lane comes into play. Teams who want visibility on work that has yet to provide value to someone (either a customer or internal team member) use the single Done lane to visualize "inventory" work. Work only moves to the Done Done lane once it has achieved its real goal.

One could argue that the Marketing team gets value from the single Done, as it signals the point where they can amp up market buzz in anticipation of the Done Done.

Customers, however, don't give a rip about the single Done. To them, a new feature isn't done until it's working right in Production. Done Done signals the real finish line, often quite awhile after the code is considered shippable or even delivered to production.

The PDCA Board

W. Edwards Deming, author of *Out of the Crisis,* is the man who, in the 1950s, taught hundreds of Japanese engineers and businessmen statistical process control (SPC) and concepts of quality. Japanese manufacturers applied his techniques and went on to experience unheard of levels of quality and productivity. Deming used an iterative, four-step approach for change, problem solving, and continuous improvement of processes and products known as *PDCA (Plan-Do-Check-Act).* For the Edwards Deming fans, Figure 31 is an example of a PDCA board design that allows you to see work flow through these iterative states.

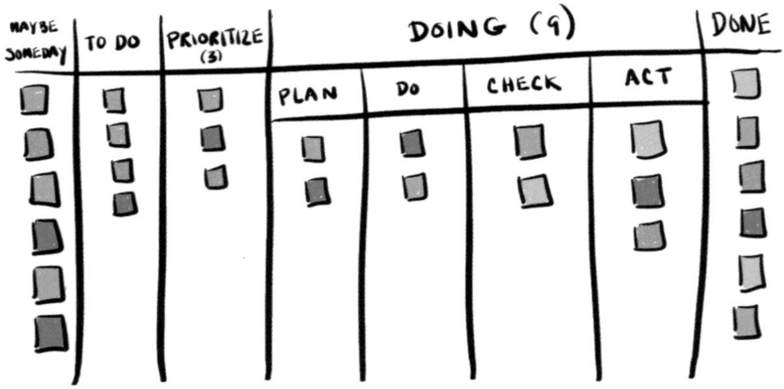

MAYBE SOMEDAY	TO DO	PRIORITIZE (3)	DOING (9)				DONE
			PLAN	DO	CHECK	ACT	

Figure 31. Plan-Do-Check-Act Board

The Home Project Board

Technology doesn't own the problem of too much WIP. Earlier in the book, I mentioned that people usually say yes to their spouses, which goes back to our desire to say yes when we like the people who ask. This prompted our home project board (Figure 32):

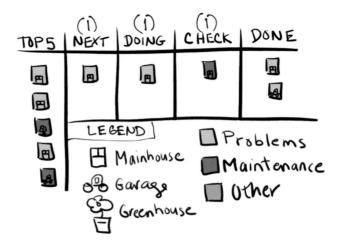

Figure 32. Home Project Board

We grouped home project work into three categories, showing problems in yellow, maintenance in green, and everything else in blue. This work flows through this simple, five lane board, which shows what our next projects are, what we're currently working on, what we've just finished doing and is being checked, and what we agree is done. The top-five column is our current priority of work. The backlog is huge and not shown here. It doesn't make sense to prioritize or even talk about the stuff in the backlog because things will likely change by the time we get to working on it.

Remember the story from earlier in the book when I asked my husband this really stupid question about building a greenhouse while he was perilously perched on top of the old crumbling outbuilding? Well, that's why we have WIP limits now in Doing and Next. You see, I can't pull in or even talk about the upcoming work until the work in Doing is in the Check column. That's a big win for the hubs. But here's what I get out of it—the hubs can't say something is done until I get to check it out. It's a win-win!

Managing Your Move

While we're on the topic of using kanban boards around the home, here is a board that Julia Wester used to manage her and her husband's most recent move (Figure 33 [1]). This one is interesting because they not only used the board to prioritize the move and track their moving progress but also took it one step further and used the cards to visualize how much each item cost, giving them visibility on the overall cost of their move.

Figure 33. Manage Your Move Board

Repetitive Tasks

There are a number of ways to visualize repetitive tasks. I'm inspired by the sequestering approach that Jim Benson and Tonianne DeMaria Barry describe in their book *Personal Kanban: Mapping Work, Navigating Life*.[2]

It's a simple, yet elegant approach designed to handle repetitive tasks that can clutter your board. I've taken the liberty to modify the design to provide a bit more data that electronic tools can provide if you are using an electronic tool versus a physical board (Figure 34).

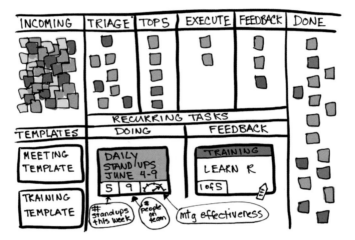

Figure 34. Repetitive Tasks

The board is split in half horizontally. Repetitive tasks are shown on the bottom half and standard work appears on the top half. Template cards are created for the repetitive work. The template card is prepopulated with all the info. All you have to do is copy the template and pop it in the doing lane. The overhead of filling out fields is gone, along with the excuse for keeping that work invisible.

The first example under "Templates" in Figure 34 is for meetings. Here, a team of nine people meet daily for a stand-up. Instead of creating a card for every stand-up, this single card sits in the Doing column for the week. The numbers on the card show the number of people in attendance (nine) along with the number of stand-up meetings (incremented for each stand-up during the week).

Similarly, a training template card can be easily copied and used again and again to keep track of all the small repetitive tasks required to do training.

Separate repetitive tasks in a dedicated area of your kanban board. It's important to keep these tasks visible because they increase WIP, and their impact should be acknowledged. Remember Operations Manager Erik from Section 2.4 who got clobbered by Thief Unplanned Work? Don't be like Erik, friends.

Purchase Order Board Design

Sometimes I think one could sail around the world in the time it takes to get a purchase order (PO) processed. Everyone I talk to who is working seriously to implement Lean thinking in their organization eventually bumps up against their accounting systems. It has become painfully clear that traditional accounting systems are restrictive and slooooooow. Finance departments are one of the last remaining holdouts in Lean transformations.

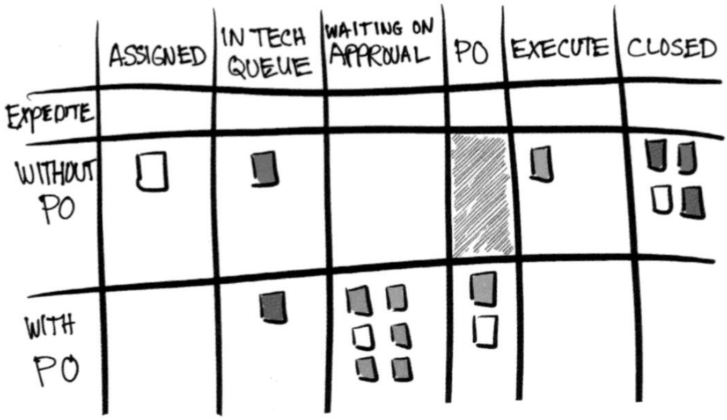

Figure 35. Purchase Order Board Design

The five time thieves make themselves at home in traditional companies that drive their business based on costs and margins. It's harder for them to steal time from Lean organizations that focus on customer and/or business value. The good news is that there are some CFOs out there who get it and are evolving from traditional project-based resource allocation and cost accounting to a faster, lower-overhead financial management model. Yippee! (For some examples, check out Brian H. Maskell, Bruce Baggaley, and Lawrence Grasso's *Practical Lean Accounting: A Proven System for Measuring and Managing the Lean Enterprise.*)

If you're still suffering from accounting woes, consider measuring the time your work waits in finance queues. (Like how long it sometimes takes to pay your favorite consultant.)

Take a look at the two horizontal swimlanes in Figure 35. One is for the work that doesn't require a PO and one is for the work that needs a PO. The Waiting on Approval and PO columns bring visibility to work that is sitting idle while waiting on Finance. Remember, the goal of kanban is to make problems visible so they can be fixed. In this example, the time the work spends waiting on Finance can be measured and used as supporting data to help your Finance department see the cost of this practice.

Likewise, professional adults struggle to keep on top of everything, yet we admonish young people when they don't. Between schoolwork, homework, chores, and extracurricular activities, students juggle many activities—some of which get lost somewhere in the calendar. This leads to a flurry of last-minute work crammed into a late night to meet the deadline. The result is a subpar experience for all involved.

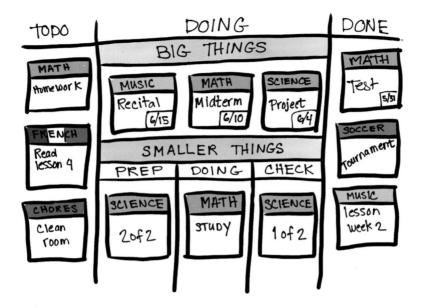

Figure 36. Student Board

The additional stress that comes with procrastination is avoidable. Instead of the out-of-sight, out-of-mind that occurs when long-term assignments are hidden on different calendar pages, make all the student things visible on one page.

Now that we've explored some of the many ways we can empower ourselves to call time thieves out into the open by making our work visible, let's take things a step further: What, for example, do we do with all this knowledge now that we've started to implement these practices? How do we prove to the higher-ups that our boards and visualizations and new practices are working? Why does this matter? Read on to find out.

- Multilevel boards provide a big-picture view of workflow across the organization as a whole.

- Small tasks may not need to be tracked on a board, but consider if adding them to the board is helpful to promote cross-training, give visibility to someone's work, or notify another team about the existence of a dependency.

- PO boards can provide the metrics needed to get buy-in on changes to traditional accounting systems.

- Kanban boards can be applied to non-work situations too! From home projects to moving to student activities, kanban brings a smooth flow to home life.

The wall of ignorance that prevents so many human beings from seeing each other clearly can only be breached by communication.
—Scott McCloud

PART

METRICS, FEEDBACK, AND CIRCUMSTANCES

It's hard to see the big picture impact when all the thieves are secretly attacking your teams at the same time.

But if we shine a light on them and expose them by tagging them, then we can use our visual senses to discover how to put these thieves out of business. To do this, I use a tool I call the Thief O'Gram. It acts as a spotlight, magnifying risky elements from exposed time theft.

How do you know how well you and your teams are doing with this? That's what Part 3 is all about. We'll cover what, why, and how to measure the health of your workflow using flow metrics.

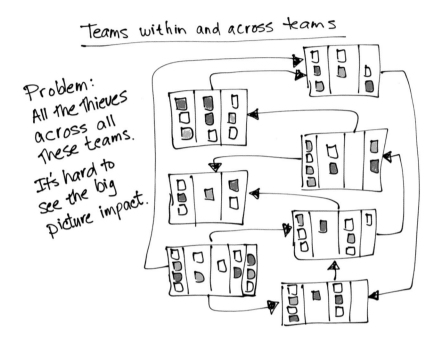

Figure 37. Teams Within Teams Board

In this part, we will discuss one of the most forgotten but important tools for communicating how the organization is doing—the operations review. It's an objective, data-driven view into the fitness of the organization, camouflaged as a lightning talk. Facilitated time-boxed conversations provide a unique space to learn from and to have pivotal discussions, as we'll see with Lean Coffee and other short but important discussions in Section 3.4. Approaches which help people enlighten us but get to the point quickly are necessary.

We don't want to give the thieves any more time to waste.

Exposing time theft is one giant step for humankind—a step that is relatively easy to take once you know where the five most wanted time thieves hide out. Now, it's time to step up the game and convert the theft damage into metrics that will allow you to deduce the risk in your system, or the uncertainty, since risk is in the eye of the beholder. Show the uncertainty, so you can do something about it, and give your next decision some ammo. But doing this requires additional skills and more information than can't be gained from blurry images in a crystal ball. Let's start with how we measure success and what drives our decisions.

Be approximately right rather than exactly wrong.
—John Tukey

3.1

YOUR METRICS
OR YOUR MONEY

Here, we're going to be using metrics to set better expectations for our customers, who always seem to be criticizing the length of time things take to complete and complaining that they can't see the progress of their requests, since making work visible is the secret to exposing the time thieves and all the havoc they wreak on you and your organization. Capturing data for metrics can help you become the voice of reason and prompt change in your organization. Metrics get attention.

Because many teams use arbitrary due dates to set expectations and then ultimately fail to hit that deadline, it's time to try a smarter approach. Namely, a probabilistic approach.

For those of you panicking at the idea of no due dates, know that they are appropriate in some situations. The characteristics that inform us of whether a due date is arbitrary or not depend on the lens that we look through.

The 2018 FIFA World Cup, scheduled to start June 14, 2018, is one such example of a real due date. So is a scheduled security audit with the federal government.

A date that the CFO selects to roll out a new CRM system so that half the Accounting team can be laid off is a suspect due date. A change to a UX enhancement? Almost certainly arbitrary. It probably does not matter that much if it ships on Tuesday or on Thursday or even next week on Monday.

If expectations are set correctly, not everything needs a due date. Being predictable is what counts. Being predicable saves time.

Becoming more predictable means we need to talk about probability and how, once we are able to shift to a more probabilistic approach, expectations around timeframes can be improved. It's all about the expectations. Setting better expectations makes leadership happy and helps make those uncomfortable stand-ups and retrospectives surprisingly fun.

Good metrics help us to see progress and understand how long things really take. This is important because the biggest complaint heard from technology customers is that things take too long. With metrics, we can demonstrate just how long things actually do take and then extrapolate on why they took so long.

Again, the problem usually starts with an arbitrary due date. That due date (often based on faulty estimates) sets the wrong expectation and then, despite all our best efforts, everything goes to hell because of conflicting priorities, unknown dependencies, and that curveball unplanned work, which always comes out of nowhere.

Everything takes longer than we think it will, especially if the work is complex. Hofstadter's Law is a statement mocking the accuracy of estimating completion for tasks with substantial complexity.[1] (It always takes longer than you expect, even when you take into account Hofstadter's Law.) We know this is true from our own experience. When you request something, how often do you receive it earlier than expected? If you frequently do, call me—I want to come work for you.

Throughout my career, no matter my role or what company, feedback from customers has invariably noted that projects take too long to complete, new features take too long to be delivered, and new cloud computing platforms take too long to get set up. Everyone wants stuff sooner than they get it, and everyone is unhappy about the delays. Yes, that is the time thieves cackling to themselves in the background as they capitalize on our distress.

The cascade of delays once a due date has been determined (often by a sales or marketing executive), usually starts with the Development team. While they begin the process thinking they have sufficient time to develop and deliver the feature, all too often they fall behind as things don't go as planned. Maybe they didn't know about the dependencies on another web team, or they didn't expect their relational database management system to be so limiting, or they hadn't planned on their core API developer getting sick. Whatever the cause, they begin to miss due dates when these unanticipated obstacles prevent them from staying on schedule.

Further delays happen in Operations, such as when a change that was promised to have zero impact on production actually does have an impact, or when the database upgrade usurps an important cross-team planning session, or when the automation engineer leaves to pursue their PhD in physics.

It's tough to make decisions about delivery timeframes and due dates in the absence of compelling evidence. A lack of data often leads to people making decisions based on opinions, which are likely to be more problematic than decisions based off of good data (i.e., visible work). Would you rather take the advice of a licensed structural engineer with ten years of seismic retrofitting experience or your brother-in-law accountant who swears that his DIY retrofit method is best? This is why metrics are so useful—they help us make good decisions.

Imagine trying to fly a plane without a fuel gauge, compass, or airspeed indicator. How risky would that be for a pilot? There's a reason for all those flight instruments in the cockpit. Without them, the pilot would have a hard time getting information about the fuel level, airspeed, and direction, which in turn would impact the flight tower as they try to guide multiple planes in for landings. Similarly, lack of visible data in IT makes us blind to problems because we don't have anything to tell us how we are actually doing. When we can't see the problems, it's hard to analyze them, which in turn makes it difficult to know what direction to take. This is what good metrics do—they steer us in the right direction.

When it comes to forecasting how long things are going to take (remember Hofstadter's Law), it's useful to look at metrics that measure progress instead of activities. Some of the best metrics that show actual progress (or lack thereof) are lead time, cycle time, WIP, and aging reports. For the rest of this section, those are the metrics we will concentrate on.

Flow Metrics

The boss (or the customer/spouse/teacher/coach) wants to know when X will be done. The way many people go about answering this question is to determine how long each step of the process will take and then add them all up. Usually, a contingency buffer is added in for good measure because things always take longer. Humans are predictably horrible at estimation, even in their area of expertise, myself included.

I estimated that the seismic retrofit my husband and I did in our basement would take four weeks—it took six weeks. We didn't consider scenarios such as how long it would take us to replace gas and water pipes in need of conversion from hard metal to flexible hoses, even though we've previously done lots of gas and water pipe work in the past.

Optimism is a near universal human trait when it comes to answering the question "When will it be done?" Software estimates are no different. Developers present optimistic estimates that management approves because of the implied achievable business targets. Furthermore, we take on *more* work because we are an optimistic bunch— it's one of the five reasons for saying yes that were mentioned in Part 1.

The problem with the traditional estimation process (add up how long each part of the process will take and then add a buffer) is that each step in a process on its way to completion is clouded with uncertainty. Each step is vulnerable to distractions from Thief Unknown Dependencies, Thief Unplanned Work, and Thief Conflicting Priorities, along with holidays, snow days, and about a million other things. Estimates are filled with more uncertainty than confidence.

The estimation process matters because, traditionally, people are held accountable for notably horrible estimates when projects fail to be delivered on time, which is most of the time. The No Estimates movement gains momentum daily as more and more projects finish late and more and more staff fail to meet their goals. What to do? Look to flow time for help.

Flow time is a measure of how long something took to do from beginning to end. You might be thinking, "Wait, that's cycle time." And you'd be right. Although—it depends on the context as to which definition you use. Depending on whom you ask, cycle time has different meanings, which I'll get to shortly. Just know that cycle time is an ambiguous term and that's why I prefer to use flow time when discussing speed metrics in general, because it is attuned with Lean. It's actually a main pillar of Lean. The term "flow time" has been around for a while—I didn't make it up.

Flow time has a start time and an end time. That's all. Flow time doesn't stop the clock just because the weekend rolls around. It doesn't do start and stop, start and stop, start and stop. What flow time does do is quantify the probability of completing x% of work in so many days.

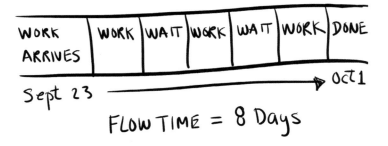

Figure 38. Flow Time Metrics

Collecting historical flow times that show, for example, that 90% of a certain type of work gets delivered within ten days allows us to say that nine out of ten times, we deliver these kinds of requests within ten days. We know then that there is a 10% probability that some work will take longer. This is important because it helps us become more predictable with our customers.

Lead time and cycle time are types of flow time metrics. They both measure duration. Using pizza order and delivery as an example, the lead time clock starts ticking when the customer orders the pizza, while the cycle time clock doesn't start ticking until the cook begins making the pizza. People who order pizza care about lead time. They want their pizza delivered quickly. Internal teams care about cycle time. They try to reduce the wait time in the delivery pipeline to be more efficient. Lean organizations optimize for speed and effectiveness.

Figure 39. Lead Time and Cycle Time

Traditionally, in a manufacturing sense, cycle time is calculated as a ratio resulting in the average time between completion of units. For our purposes, I'm defining it as the elapsed time from when you start work until the completed unit has been delivered to the customer. This is how many software technology organizations define it. Like lead time, cycle time also quantifies the probability of when work will be completed. The clock just starts ticking later. Cycle time is important because it reveals how long things take internally once work has been started. One can see how waiting on dependencies from other teams can impact the schedule.

The odds of being predictable decrease when WIP constantly increases and flow times elongate. Remember—WIP is a measure of how many different things are being juggled at the same time. Unlike most other metrics, WIP is a leading indicator. The more WIP there is in the pipeline, the longer things take to complete, period. We can look at Little's Law to understand the math behind why WIP extends completion times. Recall that lead time equals WIP over throughput. Given WIP is the numerator of that fraction, we know that when WIP goes up, so does lead time. Algebra and theory aside, the proof is in measuring the day-to-day experience.

Little's Law comes with some assumptions though. Daniel Vacanti talks about these in his book *Actionable Agile Metrics for Predictability: An Introduction*. He discusses how the true power of Little's Law lies in understanding the assumptions necessary for the law to work in the first place.[2] All metrics are based on assumptions, and Little's Law is no different. All you have to do to discredit a metric is to question the assumptions. In order for your metrics to be taken seriously, carefully consider and identify the assumptions in place.

A Training team that concentrates together on producing training materials progresses faster on the training collateral during weeks when they are not also traveling to customer sites and speaking at conferences. A Marketing team progresses faster when they work on

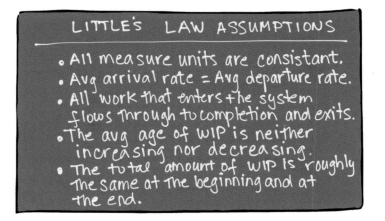

LITTLE'S LAW ASSUMPTIONS

- All measure units are consistant.
- Avg arrival rate = Avg departure rate.
- All work that enters the system
  flows through to completion and exits.
- The avg age of WIP is neither
  increasing nor decreasing.
- The total amount of WIP is roughly
  the same at the beginning and at
  the end.

seven initiatives at one time instead of thirteen. College students finish their homework sooner when they take two classes instead of three classes. One can argue that it depends on the complexity of the work. The homework for three freshman-level classes may take less time to complete than the homework for two graduate-level classes, and this is why categorizing types of work is important. When work is categorized, you can get fancy and obtain WIP reports for each work category, which in turn can improve your WIP allocations.

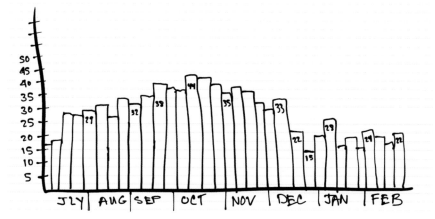

Figure 40. The WIP Report

Queuing Theory

Why do some doctor's offices always have long wait times and others don't? Is it because the busy doctors are better and have more patients? In my observation, that hasn't been the case. I've waited just as long for a crappy doctor as for good doctor. I once waited an hour for a doctor to tell me there wasn't anything I could do to improve my atrophied quad muscles after dislocating my kneecap.

I'm convinced now that the doctor's offices that don't have long wait times are the ones that understand why 100% capacity utilization doesn't work.

There is a direct correlation between WIP and capacity utilization. *Capacity utilization* is the percentage of the total possible capacity that is actually being used. If the doctor is in the office for ten hours and has ten hours of scheduled appointments, then she is considered to be fully loaded at 100% capacity utilization. If she is in the office for ten hours and has seven hours of scheduled appointments, then she is loaded at 70% capacity utilization.

What happens when a customer with a sore stomach calls and needs to be seen that day? We've all been there, right? I've been there. We're sitting in the waiting room for thirty minutes for an appointment we made two days before, when someone new walks in, checks in, and sits down. Another ten minutes pass, and the receptionist calls in the new guy before me. Those of us who have now been waiting for forty minutes roll our eyes at each other, sigh, and grumble internally about how this is forty minutes of your life you can't get back.

Attempting to load people and resources to 100% capacity utilization creates wait times. The higher utilization, the longer the wait, especially in fields with high variability, like IT.

Note that when I say "variability," I refer to a lack of consistency and how things are subject to change, such as an unexpected event. An example is when Thief Unplanned Work disrupts your deployment, and a network switch goes bad, taking out 200 or 2,000 servers. Or when someone hacks their way onto our now unsecure DB servers. Or when Brent calls in sick—and cuts in line ahead of us at the doctor's waiting room!

Unpredictable events cause variability, and the more variability, the more vulnerable we are to capacity overload. The more people and resources are utilized, the higher the cost and the risk. Computers stop responding when they get close to 100% utilization. Freeways clog up and slow way down when they are fully utilized. I like to think that good doctor's offices understand queuing theory and allow for variability for the drop-in patients. The more a person or resource is utilized, the bigger the lines (queues) get. And while it's intuitive at some level, there is some science behind it.

It's called queueing theory. When we look at the math, we can see why the single most important factor that affects queue size is capacity utilization. The reason we care about queue size is because the bigger the queue, the longer things take. What I've drawn is the curve described by the *Kingman's formula* (an approximation for the average waiting time in a queue). What it shows is the relation between utilization and wait time (Figure 41).

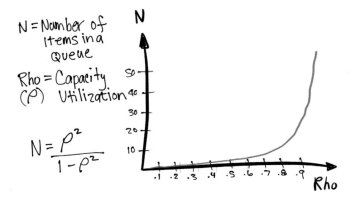

Figure 41. Queuing Theory

Queueing theory is a field of applied statistics that studies waiting lines. It allows us to quantify relationships between wait times and capacity utilization, even when arrivals and service times are highly variable. If requests arrive faster than the system can service them, they queue up.

As we move from 60–80% utilization, the queue doubles. As we move from 80–90% utilization, the queue doubles again. And again from 90–95%.[3] Once we get past 80% utilization, the queue size begins to increase almost exponentially, slowing things down to a grinding halt as it pushes 100% capacity utilization.

Have you ever worked for a company that has a 20% "creative" time policy? I've read that the main reason they do that is not for innovation (that's just a bonus) but to keep capacity utilization at 80% rather than at 100%.[4] In 1948, 3M gave its workforce 15% slack time, which years later resulted in sticky notes.[5]

We don't let our servers get to 100% capacity utilization, so let's not do that to ourselves.

Watch the Work, Not the People

Aging reports reveal how long work has been sitting in the pipeline not getting done (Figure 42). Looking at the work that's been in the system for more than sixty days (or ninety or one hundred twenty days) shines a valuable light on how much waste is in the system.

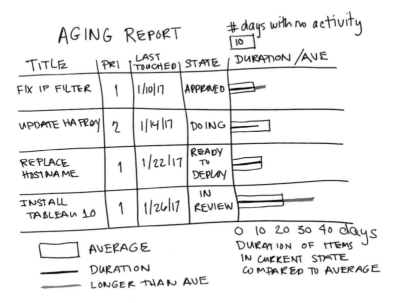

Figure 42. Aging Report

When people describe situations in the absence of compelling evidence in order to persuade others to agree with them or take some kind of action, they're relying on their own credibility. Depending on the dynamics of the team, this kind of anecdotal evidence can lead to doubt, skepticism, or even suspicion. And this is why quantitative measures are good—they are usually more accurate than personal perceptions and experiences. Good metrics help us make good decisions.

When it comes to efficiency, time is wasted when there is too much focus on resource efficiency overflow efficiency.

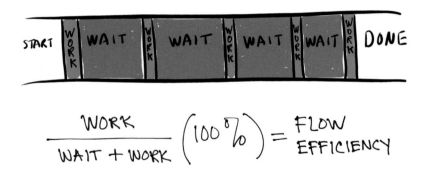

$$\frac{WORK}{WAIT + WORK}\left(100\%\right) = \begin{array}{c} FLOW \\ EFFICIENCY \end{array}$$

Figure 43. Flow Efficiency

Good metrics help others see a clearer picture and help set more accurate expectations when it comes to questions like, "When will it be done?" Due dates don't take wait time into consideration. And the problem is usually not in the process time—it's in the wait time. Focus on the wait time and not on the process time. What should the batch size of items be for delivery purposes? What is the optimal delivery rate?

There are two factors involved in this that we need to look at:

1. There is a cost from delayed feedback and from delayed release.
2. There is a cost to initially set up and work on the item, plus transaction or coordination overhead.

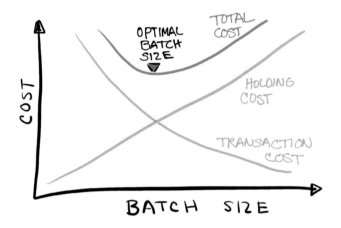

Figure 44. Optimal Batch Size

The optimal batch size for delivery then depends on the combination of the impact of economies of scale and the cost of delaying responses (holding cost and transaction cost).

Some people have a bias for large batch sizes because of the concept of economies of scale. *Economies of scale* is the cost advantage that arises with increased output of a product. The cost advantage is seen in some areas of manufacturing. Boeing produces large quantities of a single product on its assembly line. The transaction cost to create airplane engines needed for just one airplane at a time is too high, so they create a larger batch of engines at one time to reduce the associated overhead cost.

Focusing on efficiency produces better cost accounting results for large batch-size projects, such as manufacturing commercial airplane engines or publishing books. In knowledge work, however, problems with coordination costs grow nonlinearly with batch size. Old school management assumptions about economy of scale do not apply to knowledge work problems such as software development.

My little wood stove is working better for me now, even though I didn't replace it with a new, bigger stove. I changed my working routine to Pomodoro style working sessions and set a timer for thirty to forty-five minutes where I focus heads down until the ringer goes off. Enough hot coals remain in the stove that I can keep the fire going by tossing in more wood. Then I have another thirty to forty-five minutes of "don't interrupt me" time. This little break of three to five minutes helps me more than I realized.

I stand up and stretch, evaluate how much I accomplished (or didn't), and am inspired to do better with the next thirty to forty-five minutes. Previously, when working in ninety to one hundred twenty minute chunks of time, I'd let myself spend too much time on things that were not essential. The shorter window provides a sense of urgency to get something done faster, and it encourages me to break down work into smaller chunks. Ultimately, I am more efficient.

Imagine you're grocery shopping for bananas. If you buy a six-month supply of bananas at one time, your transaction cost is low, but most of the bananas will be rotten within ten days, so you've wasted money. If you buy a one-day supply of bananas at one time, they won't rot, but your transaction costs will be high, because you'll be grocery shopping every day. Somewhere in between is the right batch size of bananas.

The reduction of batch size is a critical principle of Lean manufacturing. Small batches allow manufacturers to slash work in process and accelerate feedback, which, in turn, improves cycle times, quality, and efficiency. Small batches have an even greater advantage in software development because code is hard to see and spoils quickly if not integrated into production.

One of the best predictors of short lead times is small batch sizes of work. The average amount of current WIP is directly proportional to batch size. Like WIP limits, small batch size is an enabling constraint. Work batched up in smaller sizes constrains the amount of work needed to be completed before receiving feedback. Faster feedback makes for a better outcome.

Small batch sizes enable fast and predictable lead times in most value streams, which is why there is a relentless focus on creating a smooth and even flow of work.

When you can implement the practices above in your work and life and show how these practices save you time, money, and stress through metrics, you are more able to proactively banish the time thieves from your sphere.

KEY TAKEAWAYS

- Delays are common; use metrics, particularly flow metrics, to help you make good decisions on priorities, WIP limits, and capacity utilization.

- Stop letting yourself and your team reach 100% capacity utilization.

- Look for the optimal batch size to help you achieve efficiency while keeping transaction costs down.

○○○○○

Invest energy in collecting metrics that help you make decisions.
—Eric Ries

3.2

THE TIME
THIEF O'GRAM

Ladies and gents, I give you the Time Thief O'Gram.

Think of this tool as a spotlight, shining a light on a criminal lineup of the uncertainty across your organization.

The intent here is to look at metrics that reveal high risk. Common metrics such as the number of story points completed over a period of time (*velocity*), the number of bugs that escaped into production, or the number of deployments to production don't reveal very much about risk.

I'm going to argue here that time theft should be measured by the things that cause the problems in the first place and prevent your teams from delivering quality work quickly: too much WIP, unplanned work, neglected work, conflicting priorities, and unknown dependencies. These are the causes behind mediocre work done too slowly.

Each of these time thieves can be captured using work item types and card tags or a combination of both. If we can count these things and measure them, we can see both the stolen time and which thief stole it. It's good to know if Thief Unplanned Work did it in the kitchen with the knife or if it was Thief Too Much WIP in the library with the candlestick. The Time Thief O'Gram shows who committed the crime and reveals how much was stolen.

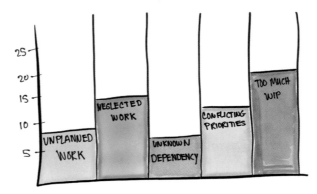

Figure 45. The Original Time Thief O'Gram

The Time Thief O'Gram can be generated by tagging all your thieves on your kanban board. In this example, each thief has been color coded to make it even more visual. Once you have all these tagged, you can visualize, count, and track them week over week or month over month. In doing so, you can begin to see patterns and connections that would otherwise be scattered across multiple team boards.

We can look at the congregated Time Thief O'Gram (Figure 46) to compare thieves and their trends week over week to see the fluctuation in the amount of too much WIP across all the teams over time.

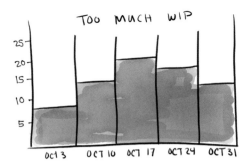

Figure 46.
Congregated Time
Thief O'Gram

There is, of course, a variety of ways to make time thievery visible. Figure 47 shows a balanced scorecard to help people determine which thieves to focus on first, which ones they are doing well with, and which ones are robbing them of time and predictability. Tracking and measuring these thieves puts people in a position to do something about them.

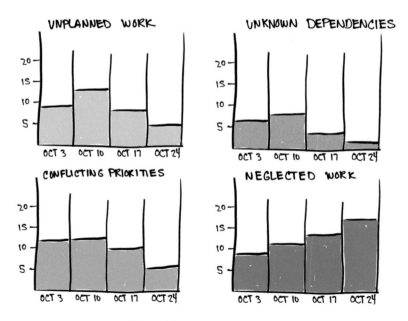

Figure 47. Balanced Scorecard

In my work, I am frequently asked about the best way to influence the CIO to use a DevOps/Lean/kanban/whatever approach. The CIOs I've talked to want two things: less risk and more predictability. The Time Thief O'Gram shows you that. It shows risk (*ahem* uncertainties) with respect to unplanned work, neglected work, conflicting priorities, and unknown dependencies. The Time Thief O'Gram also shows when WIP exceeds limits (based on the team's own set WIP limits). Because WIP is a leading indicator, tracking WIP levels can signal problems early and warn you that things are going to take longer than expected. If predictability for delivering on time is important, then what would it be worth to your CIO to have this kind of transparency? Effective communication requires key messages from different sources. Look to the Time Thief O'Gram as one consistent source of important messages.

KEY TAKEAWAYS

- The Time Thief O'Gram reveals which thieves are at work in your organization and how much they are stealing.
- The metrics from the Time Thief O'Gram provide transparency for leaders eager to see the issues facing teams. These are an excellent source for getting executive buy-in to do the things necessary to improve predictability and reduce risk.

Let the flow manage the processes, and not let management manage the flow. —Taiichi Ohno

3.3

OPERATIONS REVIEW

David Anderson introduced us to operations reviews at Corbis. Everyone on his management team had to present their team's metrics. It was my first experience as a team lead presenting metrics to a group of more than thirty people. I was terrified standing in the conference room: my voice shook, my heart pounded, and I thought I was going to maybe throw up. What if my presentation let the team down?

This experience taught me that management responsibilities include knowing the demand on my team and being able to present what the demand looked like in relation to the capability of the team to meet the demand.

Figure 49 is a cumulative flow diagram (CFD)—a stacked line chart that shows the amount of WIP and items delivered over time. I presented this CFD monthly at the operations review on behalf of the Build and Release team. When June rolled around, incoming requests spiked, and because I was able to demonstrate this spike, my request for more headcount was approved.

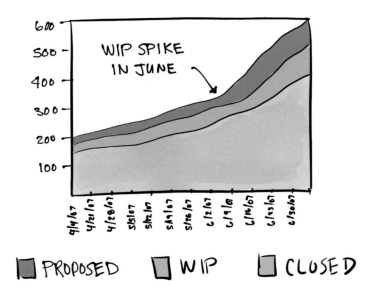

Figure 48. Cumulative Flow Diagram for Ops Review

The goal of the recurring monthly operations reviews is to collectively look at the data to see and understand the health of the organization. A disciplined and consistent review of organizational health provides a great opportunity for continuous improvement. Operations reviews provide feedback loops to help you understand how the organization is doing and to enable you to make sound decisions concerning your next move. They are objective data-driven retrospectives on the organization's performance.

The reviews are organization-wide and involve senior leaders, managers, leads, and individual contributors to communicate that the organization takes performance seriously by setting an expectation for objective, data-driven, quantitative management. In other words, operations reviews are one way in which we can make work more visible by seeing what has come before.

Here are some logistics for how to run a successful operations review: Each manager has five minutes to present their team's metrics for the month. Allow two to three minutes for questions or comments from the audience. Time-boxing the presentations and the following question and answer session helps keep people focused on what's important, gives speakers their fair share of time, and avoids going off track or consuming too much time. Time-boxing avoids the common problem that occurs when you give someone a mic and can't get them off the stage.

Sample operations review agenda:
- Opening remarks from leadership.
- Presentations from team leads or front line managers.
- Closing remarks.

Metrics to Present

In order to understand how we are doing, what the risks are, and how to improve predictability, Ops reviews show how the teams actually performed the previous month against promises/expectations.

When beginning operations reviews, the suggestion is for each lead to report on the following metrics and data for the first few months:
1. **Throughput:** Throughput is how many things were completed over a period of time. One way to show throughput is with a CFD. The CFD will also show the ratio of incoming requests against completed requests and the amount of WIP at each stage of the workflow.
2. **Flow time:** Look at how long it took items to move across the board from the time work was pulled into an in-progress column through delivery. The visual (hopefully a report easily generated by your workflow tool) shows the actual flow time for *each* completed work

item for the previous month. This is useful for learning so you can make changes to your processes, your system, or to decrease variability and increase predictability. Or, if the card size is similar in nature, we may find it interesting to calculate the average cycle time or lead time.

3. **Issues and blocked work items:** Identify any major issues or blocked work that is preventing the team from making progress. This will help people understand why things took so long and know what changes are underway to prevent those problems from happening again.

4. **The Time Thief O'Gram:** Select one or more time thieves to report on to expose their theft.

Additional metrics you may want to consider presenting:

- Aging reports
- Card type distribution
- Failure load (value demand versus failure demand) as a measure of quality
- Flow efficiency

Future Operations Reviews

For each metric, we want to track the trend over time so we can see the improvements (or not). If we are to demonstrate continuous improvement, we want the mean trend to improve over time. To demonstrate predictability, we want the spread of variation to decrease over time. For example, to demonstrate that one can predictably arrive to work on time, it helps when the frequency of late arrivals decreases over time and the length of the lateness shrinks.

Another example: Amtrak has a passenger train from Portland to Seattle that is supposed to run on a set schedule throughout the day. According to the schedule, the last train of the day is supposed to arrive in Seattle at 8:05 p.m. Sometimes the train arrives at 8:25 p.m. Other times it arrives at 2:30 a.m. So, the train is unpredictable. The wide spread in arrival time causes variation in the train system.

The variable arrival times are caused by several factors. For example, our rainy Pacific Northwest weather generates unpredictable landslides, blocking trains until the rails are cleared (Thief Unplanned Work). Furthermore, because freight trains have a higher priority than passenger trains, and there are only so many train tracks that run through the tunnel, the Amtrak train takes a backseat to the freight trains (Thief Conflicting Priorities).

In order for Amtrak to demonstrate predictability, they would need to address landslides and change prioritization policies to decrease the variation of arrival times of the train from Portland to Seattle.

These are the types of decisions that operations reviews make possible. Without good, objective metrics, it is very difficult to understand exactly how the various thieves steal away our time and energy. But by making work visible, we are able to see the patterns and communicate to our organizations just where the problems lie, so we can learn and adjust and improve.

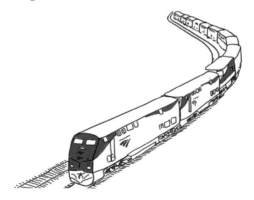

KEY TAKEAWAYS

- Operations reviews are an opportunity to present objective metrics that can form a foundation for improvement.

- Use time-boxing to keep operations reviews and speakers from running long.

- Good metrics for operations reviews include throughput, flow time, and time theft along with issues and blocked items.

- Track metrics over time so that you can see what improvements have been made or still need to be made.

Friction around priorities and practices happens on the way to improvement. —Scott Nasello

3.4

THE ART OF THE MEETING

Wednesday, Seattle, 9:00 a.m.

Nine people sip coffee around a table at a South Lake Union coffee shop in Seattle. All eyes are on Carmen, who is making a point about the impact of the latest round of layoffs at his company. The group is discussing how reorganizations impact different teams. People politely wait for Carmen to finish his sentence before voicing their opinion. A minute later, a timer goes off, and after a simple vote from everyone at the table, the subject changes to the next visually queued up topic written on a sticky note, "How to influence leadership."

This is Lean Coffee—a structured meeting with few rules. Participants gather, build an agenda, and begin talking.

Created by Jim Benson and Jeremy Lightsmith in 2009, Lean Coffee emerged as one of the greatest ways a group of people can discuss ideas.[1] The conversations are productive because the agenda for the meeting is democratically generated. People are engaged because they get to talk about topics that matter to them. Lean Coffee works because attendees are in charge of the agenda and everyone's voice is heard. The minimal rules combined with mutual respect for each other provides a setting that encourages open dialogue and collaboration. Adam Yuret, who wrote *How to Have Great Meetings: A Lean Coffee Book,* says,

> *Lean Coffee turns traditional, one-direction management meetings on its head by helping teams uncover the most important topics to the majority of people, by allowing everyone to hear and to be heard, and by providing real-time feedback.*[2]

I will add to that by saying that Lean Coffee doesn't just change the tone of team meetings, it shifts the overall culture within the enterprise using it.

Reversing conditions where time thieves thrive requires change. Many of the problems related to time thievery have to do with organizational problems or company culture. To put it another way, when the company has a culture that is focused on keeping people busy (instead of on keeping work flowing), it invariably results in overloading people with too much WIP. This is not a productive culture. We want to avoid the mistake of having a goal to keep people busy all the time when the goal should be to generate value for the business.

In order for change to occur, people's behaviors must change, and in order to change behavior, the hearts and minds of people must be open to change. Casual, in-person conversations with someone with an opposing viewpoint is one of the easiest paths to changing someone's mind. Nothing accomplishes this better than a personal relationship generated by face-to-face conversation in a safe, calm, and respectful setting such as Lean Coffee.

How to Lean Coffee

My experience facilitating Lean Coffees since 2012 has led me to develop a decent plan of action for getting them going within your team or organization.

First, block off sixty to ninety minutes.

Next, gather up sticky notes and markers and place them around a table. Once everyone is seated, review the Lean Coffee rules: only one person speaks at a time, and participants should attempt to listen more than they talk.

Then, invite participants to take just two to three minutes and use the provided materials to jot down as many topics as they would like, but instruct them to write only one topic per sticky note (sticky notes are our friends!). After everyone is done writing, participants should briefly (two sentences are usually sufficient) summarize their own topic(s) for the group so others can understand what they are voting on. Each participant gets two votes. It's okay to vote on your own topic(s). It's okay to use both votes on a single topic or distribute them across two different topics.

Tally the votes to prioritize the topics. Then, run the topics through a kanban board right on top of the table. Three columns are essential: To Discuss, Discuss, and Done. Place the topic with the highest number of votes in the Discuss column, and sort the others in priority order in the To Discuss column. If you wish, you may create a fourth column for decisions, epiphanies, or actions.

Set a timer for five minutes and invite the author of the topic in the Discuss column to lead off the discussion. The facilitator should take care to ensure everyone has a chance to speak. (Beware the loud extrovert monopolizing the conversation!) When the alarm goes off, allow the speaker to finish their current sentence, then vote using thumbs up or down. A majority of thumbs-up votes means the discussion may continue for additional minutes. A majority of thumbs down votes signals the group to move on to the next topic. The facilitator can break any ties.

Repeat this process until the Lean Coffee session ends. Lean Coffee concludes with a round of closing comments from each participant. It's okay to pass.

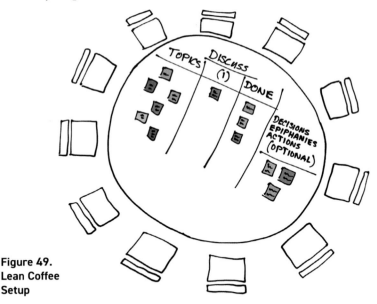

**Figure 49.
Lean Coffee
Setup**

While Lean Coffee usually occurs with just a small group of people, don't be constrained by group size. I've facilitated Lean Coffees with fifteen to twenty tables of ten people each.

Stand-Ups

Earlier, I described stand-ups that saw more foot shuffling than discussion, where project managers tried unsuccessfully to get status from attendees. A ceremony where you go around the room and everyone says what they're working on today, what they did yesterday, and what they plan on doing tomorrow is a status meeting, which is unnecessary when work is visible on a board. It's also boring. When we go around the room, people spend the time figuring out what to say when it's their turn instead of giving others their full attention.

When the stand-up is done in front of a visual board, it is obvious what people are working on. When it comes to the stand-up, get to the point. Is there anything blocked? Is there any invisible work? Is there something we should know about? Something that will impact us? Something that should be on the board, but it isn't? Make it snappy, and get to the after stand-up, where real problems get solved.

At one company I worked at, a group of thirty-five people met daily at 9:30 a.m. for stand-ups. Initially, the "go around the room" process was used. Some people were so uncomfortable speaking in the spotlight that their voices were mere whispers. Other people enjoyed being in the limelight and tended to hog a lot of precious and expensive time. Imagine the cost of thirty-five engineers and managers being in an ineffective meeting, not to mention that listening to thirty-five people report their status made for a dreadfully boring meeting. So, the meeting rules changed. Instead of going around the room, we set a policy that the board must be updated and accurate prior to 9:00 a.m. This allowed people to simply look at the board to see the latest status, and the stand-up could be spent focusing on risk and uncertainty.

The following three questions became the new agenda:

1. **What work is blocked?** Notice the emphasis is on the work and not the person. Thief Unknown Dependencies often chimed in here with blockages due to database architecture issues.

2. **What work is at risk of becoming blocked?** Here's where Thief Conflicting Priorities typically showed up.

3. **Is there work being done that isn't on the board?** This question would then evolve to include queries about work that might currently be invisible to the team or problems that might have occurred during production the previous night. These questions often revealed the dirty work of Thief Unplanned Work.

This change allowed the team to immediately see and recognize major blockers preventing important work from being delivered. The three questions made the stand-up simple and fast. It was over by 9:45 a.m. (just fifteen minutes), and this allowed an amazing thing to happen that was completely unexpected and spontaneous. Engineers hung around after the stand-up (because they had fifteen minutes free before heading off to their next meeting) and started to tackle some of the engineering problems that blocked work. We called this time the "after stand-up." Previously, I would have had to schedule a meeting eight days out in order to find available time on the engineers' calendars and to find an available meeting room (meeting room real estate was in high demand, and people frequently had to go to the coffee shop around the corner to meet).

The result was that meetings decreased because people hung around afterwards to solve the problems that had just been discussed. Half past the hour is a good time to schedule a fifteen minute stand-up because when it's over, people will have fifteen minutes before they have to get to their next meeting.

Interruptions also decreased because instead of people popping in and interrupting me with "Got five minutes?" they knew that they could catch me at after the stand-up to ask timely questions or get quick feedback.

The stand-up together with the after stand-up allowed us to reveal where the time thieves were at work, which in turn saved much time from being stolen.

One last comment on the topic of meetings is the acknowledgment that the regular cadence of a meeting held at the same time, in the same location is extremely helpful for all involved. This relatively simple guideline reduced uncertainty for thirty-five expensive people.

And now, in the next section, we turn our attention to practices that I consider problematic. These practices range from isolated occurrences to commonplace misfortunes, but they all hinder us in our pursuit of keeping our work visible and holding the thieves at bay.

mon	tue	wed	thur	fri
9:30 - 9:45 standup	9:30 - 9:45 stand up	9:30 - 9:45 standup	9:30 - 9:45 stand up	9:30 - 9:45 stand up
	1:1 with Sarah	Value stream Integration training	All Hands	events planning
Weekly sales mtg	platform demo		Marketing presentation	
office hours				4-6pm Happy hour at HQ

KEY TAKEAWAYS

- Lean Coffee allows people to discuss the topics they want in a fun, respectful, and efficient setting.

- Organize and flow Lean Coffee topics through a kanban once they have been voted on.

- Using a board to show the status of work allows stand-up time to be spent discussing problems and uncovering invisible work.

- Holding stand-ups at a regular cadence at the same location reduces uncertainty.

Tell me how you measure me and I'll tell you how I'll behave.
—*Eliyahu Goldratt*

3.5

BEASTLY PRACTICES

I decided to throw this section in as we near the end because there are some things that must be said in the spirit of full disclosure, but I didn't want to scare you away with my opinionated messages at the beginning. Nonetheless, I wanted to include them so you and your team members will recognize them when you see them—a kind of red flag cheat sheet of company practices that might be negatively impacting the work place.

So, listed in no particular order are my rants and other musings that incite particularly visceral reactions. They concern systemic pressures that occur throughout the organization. These are the pressures that lay the foundation for Thief Too Much WIP and other thieves to sabotage improvements and, in some cases, jeopardize the emotional and psychological safety of the workforce (which in turn makes people update their résumés and search for healthier and kinder workplace climates).

Flow Time Metrics that Exclude Weekends

There are three reasons why excluding weekends from speed metrics is a big problem.

1. **All metrics are based on assumptions.** And all you need to do to discredit a metric is to question the assumptions. Allow me to demonstrate. Are you saying you never work weekends? What about holidays? What about vacation days? Should we count the vacation days people qualify for or only the ones taken? What if we just look at the time people worked? Does everyone always work a forty-hour week? How much time are you willing to spend debating assumptions in order to make your metrics credible?

2. **Flow time exclusions encourage gaming of the data.** What happens when resource utilization decisions are made based off of timesheets? How accurate are those estimates? When people work weekends but don't count that time, the metrics can be deceptively reassuring. Furthermore, I've watched workers attribute 100% of their time to a single project because they feared that it would otherwise reflect poorly on them. The data was wrong and everyone knew it. Using metrics to shame people encourages gaming. The same thing is true with target-driven metrics. When the focus is on the metric instead of the goal, it's a problem. If people don't reveal things to us, then we lose transparency.

3. **Business customers care about duration.** If you're my customer and I tell you something will be done in thirty days but then don't deliver in thirty days because I was only counting working days, you're not going to be happy. Customers don't care how long their thing sat in development or test. They want to know about the duration.

There will always be variability in our systems due to weekends, holidays, unplanned work, and sick days. Credit leadership for being bright enough to know that requests arriving the day before a three-day weekend will have a longer lead time. Visibility of accurate metrics helps us make good decisions but is dependent on the transparency of others. Help others be okay with the truth. If you want more predictability in your organization, measure flow time accurately. Once you exclude weekends from flow time, or any other time people aren't thought to be working, you open the door to many questioned assumptions.

Ineffective Accounting Methods with Time Sheets

Correlating activity with business value is risky. High activity levels do not equate to high business value. High activity levels equate to hidden queues, which contribute to teams finishing projects late. Using a time sheet to track the number of hours Todd spent working on a task does not reflect the speed of delivered business value. Furthermore, the customer doesn't care how many hours Todd spent working on line item 236.

I've experienced these problems first hand. I once waited eight weeks for a purchase order from a customer who wanted me to train their team within three weeks, and another time I waited twelve weeks to be added to a company's payment system. The processes used in traditional accounting systems do not seem to be able to move as quickly as other parts of the business need them to. Some organizations are turning the tables on ineffective accounting methods that are based on costs and margins by focusing instead on the business value created and the economic profitability of the value stream.

With other viable options available, organizations that are bleeding from budget process landmines can turn the tables and staunch the wounds by looking into other methods, such as those offered up by Brian H. Maskell, Bruce Baggaley, and Larry Grasso in their book *Practical Lean Accounting: A Proven System for Measuring and Managing the Lean Enterprise.*

Gantt Charts

Like a false promise, Gantt charts (jokingly called "can't charts" by some) fool us into believing that timeline accuracy based off estimates is doable. Developed by Henry Gantt in the 1910s, a *Gantt chart* is a type of horizontal bar chart that illustrates the start and finish dates of all the tasks in a project. The problem is that Gantt charts don't consider the wait and blocked times that occur due to high capacity utilization of workers.

Gantt charts subdivide project tasks into time intervals that get broken down into smaller groups of subtasks. Due dates are identified, and people are incentivized to meet the timeline. One can recognize this in the promise, "If project V gets done by July first, you can take two days off during the week of the Fourth of July!"

In response, people insert contingency buffers into the plan to prevent tasks from missing their deadline, and these aggregate into even longer timelines with more variability. Each contingency buffer opens the door to including more work. "Oh, that's not due until Thursday. Can we add this other little fix in?"

Each bucket in the timeline is already prone to some kind of variance. For example, someone goes off to a two-day conference or takes their car into the shop, the internet connectivity goes down, or the database server is running slowly.

When we add in contingency buffers, we unintentionally extend the timeline even further because the workers with the highest demand get blocked and aren't there when you need them, or it takes them longer to respond because project V isn't the only thing they're working on (a likely scenario if they're in high demand). As a result, there is work not getting done until someone with the right skill set has capacity to do it. So we wait.

We wait while flow time goes up, other tasks dependent on that task get delayed, and people start asking, "Is it done? Is it done? Is it done?" More project statuses get requested, more variability creeps in, and costs go up. This includes psychological costs, which go up because as queues and wait times get longer, they thwart motivation. When something is ready to use within an hour, there is a sense of urgency. When it's a three week wait, there is little value in hurrying to finish it. The work begins to decay like perishable fruit when it sits around for too long. Partially completed work can be very expensive.

Instead of managing work with Gantt charts, consider managing work with queues. We know the longer the queue, the longer the wait time. The focus on queues and wait times changes the game. Projects no longer need to be accomplished by heroic, sleep-deprived people driven by Gantt charts.

Instead of giving due dates, reduce WIP, prioritize by CoD, and reduce batch size. Instead of organizing by projects, organize by product and decouple dependencies on architecture or single threaded skill sets that increase wait times and lengthen queues.

Individually Named Swimlanes

Figure 50 shows the results of a team subjected to begrudgingly using their boss's kanban board design.

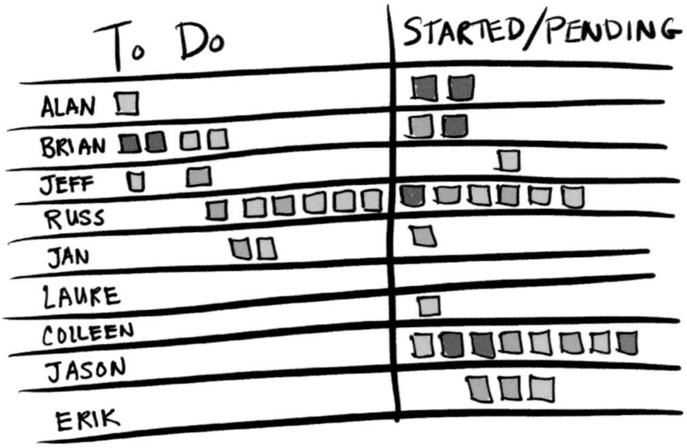

Figure 50. Individually Named Swimlanes

The boss mandated this board design, carving out swimlanes for individual team members. He wanted visibility on what his team was working on. It's not difficult to understand why the team hated it. Here are some of the problems.

There are four main problems with individually named swimlanes. Given a constantly changing environment, there is a desire to feel in control of your own work, but there are costs to this desire:

1. Because the board design was focused on individuals, stand-ups focused on individuals instead of the work itself. The stand-up became an "I" fest. "I did this," and "I'm doing that," and "I'm going to do this other thing." Keep the spotlight on the work, not the people.

2. There was a perception of poor performance when some people didn't move tickets across the board as fast as others. Not all work is the

same. Some work is more plagued by time thieves than other work is. Unplanned work can inflate tasks and cause variation. (Remember the impact of landslides on train schedules?)

3. People felt they couldn't touch work outside their lane. Instead of being encouraged to broaden toward T-shaped skills (Figure 51), they concentrated on greater specialization, which made Thief Unknown Dependencies happier.

4. Focusing on utilization prevented collaboration. People were incentivized to not help others. Why should Alan go help Russ if it means the work in Alan's lane will take longer to complete? People will prioritize based on making themselves look good. This behavior can decrease business value. It could be that the single most beneficial thing Alan could do to increase business value is to go help Russ finish something.

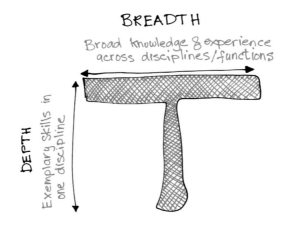

Figure 51. T-Shaped Skills

If this is your situation, and you want to take an incremental step in a direction that moves you closer to optimizing the flow of work, then consider a board design that brings visibility to the nature of the demand and to the skill sets required to get the job done (Figure 52). This way, when work is stalled, it's easier to see which skill is in high demand and work to cross train more people to reduce the risk of bottlenecks. Instead of trying to keep individuals busy, change how you visualize the work to inspire how to focus on the right thing—smoothing the flow of work from start to finish.

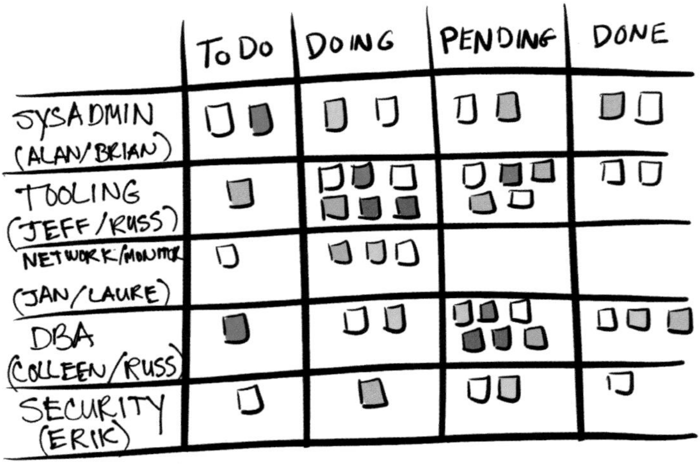

	To Do	Doing	Pending	Done
SYSADMIN (ALAN/BRIAN)	▯▮	▯ ▯	▯ ▮	▮▯
TOOLING (JEFF/RUSS)	▮	▮▮▯ ▮▮▮	▯▮▮ ▮▯	▯ ▯
NETWORK/MONITOR (JAN/LAURE)	▯	▮ ▯▯		
DBA (COLLEEN/RUSS)	▮	▯ ▯	▯▯▯ ▮▮▮	▯▯ ▮
SECURITY (ERIK)	▯	▮	▯▯	▯

Figure 52. Specialization

Work Scattered Everywhere

Meetings can be hard enough on their own. Just making sure the right people show up at the right time to discuss the right topics to hopefully achieve the correct outcome is a difficult task. Add in three different boards, six spreadsheets, four slack channels, a video conference tool with poor video conferencing bandwidth, twenty-seven open browsers, and umpteen other tools and apps, and you've plunged into meeting malaise. Who wants to juggle all that chaos? No one who wants to kick the time thieves in the butt, that's for sure. Keep things simple so people waste less time searching for information. Time spent searching increases WIP.

Garish Card Colors

Information/data can be beautiful to gaze upon, but not when surrounded by colors that are at visual war with each other or with the background. Beauty attracts. Design your visual kanban user experience with beauty in mind. Author of three bestselling books on visualizing information and TED talk speaker David McCandless identifies four elements he believes are necessary for a visualization to work:

- **Information:** The data must have integrity and must be accurate.
- **Function:** The goal must be useful and efficient.
- **Visual form:** The metaphor must have *beauty* and structure.
- **Story:** The concept must be interesting and relevant.[1]

Make boards visually appealing to keep people interested and engaged and to avoid confusion and wasted time. Communication can be hard when many different tools are used. Improve communication with elegant visuals that integrate well with other tools.

Best Practices

It was in Honolulu while working at Boeing that I heard someone (my boss, actually) say, "Do it right the first time." I instinctively knew that wasn't right. The only time anyone does anything right the first time is when they follow directions given by someone else who has done it many times before. The first time doing anything is an experiment. And so it is with kanban. The first board design attempt is an experiment to help you discover how to improve your workflow. That's why there really are no "best practices" when it comes to designing your kanban board, as well as many other situations. Unless you are doing something simple that has been done many times before—something where cause and effect are known, we cannot know exactly what specifically should be done. We just don't know what we don't know yet.

Today, when I hear the term "best practices," I attempt to use my magic introvert powers to avoid physically cringing. I have to remind myself that there are appropriate times for best practices. When the pilot goes through the checklist before heading down the runway. When the nurse cleans a wound before applying a bandage. When the system admin pulls the server out of rotation before restarting IIS. Best practices might sound cringeworthy, but they do have their place, especially when you're doing something routine but important.

Now that my ranting is done, let's head to the conclusion of our journey together, where we'll answer a tough question, look at improving alignment, and reduce resistance to change.

> note to Self:
>
> If relationship between cause & effect is well known And the team is experienced, then ok- apply a best practice.
>
> In complicated situations, different options for solving the same problem exist (depending on which expert you ask), hence- there are multiple "good practices" to choose from.
>
> But, when cause & effect are unknown, There IS NO BEST PRACTICE!

KEY TAKEAWAYS

- Don't exclude times when people aren't "supposed" to be working from metrics or the metrics will be skewed.

- Look for alternatives to ineffective accounting methods. Just because they are "the way things have always been done," doesn't mean they represent the only (or best) way to do them.

- Consider replacing Gantt charts with queues.

- Beware of individually named swimlanes.

- Simplify meeting tools whenever possible.

- Make kanban boards (and other presentation materials) visually appealing to engage viewers.

- Best practices have their place, particularly when it comes to simple routine tasks, but it's often a better idea to conduct your own experiments to discover what truly works for your situation and organization.

CONCLUSION: CALIBRATION

Never let formal education get in the way of your learning.
—*Mark Twain*

Mountain View, California, September 2011

Following the first ever Kanban for DevOps class in Mountain View, California, a man sporting a kilt and long locks asked, "How do you integrate kanban with ticket systems without slowing down high-throughput Ops teams?" The man, whose name was Ben, wrote the question on a large, orange sticky note while standing at the back of the DevOps meetup room.

Now, looking at the orange note, which I saved, I remember that I didn't know how to answer the question at the time. It's as valid a question today as it wasin 2011. My response today begins with one comment and two questions: My comment is that any change, even a good change, impacts performance. Adding new people to the team requires some level of on-boarding and getting people up to speed. In the short term, the team will be impacted. But is it worth it? There has to be some win in order to disrupt the team. Next, my two questions are:

1. Why do you need kanban if your teams already have high throughput?
2. What's the problem that you want to make visible?

I would have to make a lot of assumptions to spit out an answer worth much. But for the sake of it, let's assume that while the team has high throughput, they are overloaded and rely on heroics to meet their demand. The problem you want to make visible in this scenario would be the overwhelming demand your team is having to work through (Thief Too Much WIP) and the reason why it's like that. Making this visible allows you to see the problem and have a think about what to do next. The answer could be to reduce WIP and reprioritize. It could also be to bring in more people to manage WIP (and to keep your current people from seeing greener pastures).

Limiting WIP can keep throughput high while reducing the level of demand as well as the problems that create and then feed into that demand, such as constant interruptions from unplanned work and burned-out team members.

This is what we've been talking about throughout this book: limiting the time thieves' ability to mess with your life by exposing them, and then continuously improving on ineffective practices across teams, departments, and organizations to reap maximum benefits. Remember, exposing the time thieves is important because it's ridiculously hard to manage invisible work. When there is too much WIP, there is no time to simply think.

When we look at time theft we can narrow it down to calibration because that's what making work visible does. When you can see the thieves for what they are, it allows you to realign and calibrate the systemic issues that hinder your organization.

Alignment (Coherence) of Technical and Business Teams

Aligning technical and business teams is a matter of gaining clarity and consensus around *why* teams are doing what they're doing. Your teams may (and in fact, should) argue about the *who*, *what*, and *when*, but the context around *why* should be well understood. Alignment problems are often related to conflicting priorities resulting from too much demand. If all requests got done, there would be no problem. Priorities conflict because there is too much WIP.

Gaining crystal clear understanding on why a company is in business in the first place can fundamentally transform the culture of an organization because leaders can go back to this to make priority decisions.

Change is hard for humans and is often met with resistance, especially during dramatic transformations. Lean coaches refer to this as the J-curve (Figure 53). Big changes cause dips in performance due to a variety of reasons: learning new material, hiring more people, installing and using new tools, yada, yada, yada. That's why small, gradual changes are easier to implement. Small change meets with less defiance. Take eBay for example.

One day, eBay designers decided that a bright yellow background wasn't cool anymore, so they replaced it with a white one. Customers didn't like it one bit. So many people complained that eBay rolled the change back to yellow. Then, over a period of several months, they

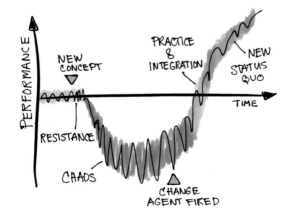

**Figure 53.
The J Curve**

modified the background color one shade of yellow at a time, until all the yellow was gone and had been replaced with white.[1] Hardly a single user noticed. This is the power of gradual change—it gets met with less resistance as people are only asked to adapt to one small piece at a time rather than to everything all at once. Satisfy people with gradual change instead of dramatic change.

Other challenges with rolling out a new way of working:

1. Limiting WIP is scary and not intuitive. Limiting WIP means people can't say yes all the time, and this makes them uncomfortable. But if WIP limits are ignored, think through what will happen to your flow time and chaos levels. Select a WIP limit that is doable but challenges you to say no some of the time.

2. There's always more demand than capacity. Be wary of falling back into the old habit of starting everything because of the pressure to say yes to everything. Remember, WIP limits are your friend and the key to getting the most important work done.

3. People who are afraid may not cooperate with the level of visualization you are seeking. Leadership should strive to relieve the fear, so people are comfortable with transparency. Don't punish the people; change the system.

How you can veer off course:

1. Focusing too much internally and not enough on interactions with stakeholders/customers. Strike a balance. Remember the cost of delay to the business when prioritizing your work.

2. Never finishing because you want it to be perfect. You are going to keep improving. A completed blog post is better than no blog post. Deliver something so you can get feedback as soon as possible.

3. Trying to fix everything at once. Visualize your current reality

and then make small adjustments so you can measure the impact of each change and learn from it.

4. Expecting overnight results. It can take months for a kanban design to stabilize. Even then, you will be continually improving. There is always room for improvement.

As a Lean coach, I often get asked what the difference is between kanban and *Scrum* (an Agile framework used to complete projects). They are both Agile methods that use constraints to enable productive outcomes.

Scrum and kanban can work well together. They are more alike than they are different. Differences include release cadence, roles, and the type of constraints themselves. Scrum uses a time-box (usually two weeks) to limit demand, while kanban uses the WIP limit to constrain demand. Some teams use a hybrid of both and call it ScrumBan (originally designed as a way to transition from Scrum to kanban).

I am inspired by Klaus Leopold and Siegfried Kaltenecker who wrote a kanban elevator pitch in their book *Kanban Change Leadership: Creating a Culture of Continuous Improvement.*

> *Kanban is a method for the continuous improvement of your own area of work. You don't begin with a big change management project, but rather focus on a series of small change steps. You identify the most important business partners and together investigate the strengths and weaknesses in your current work processes. Based on visualization of these processes, you use a simple means to make things more efficient, improve lead times and create added value for your customers.*[2]

To investigate strengths and weaknesses with business partners, using visualization reduces resistance to change in the organization. Making work visible helps with investigation, which in turn helps people become comfortable with change.

Old school language tends to block progress. Combatting time thieves takes agility, daring, and new words to describe new ways of doing things. Think *people* (not resources), *good practices* (not best practices), and *uncertainty* (not exactness).

Changing how we work requires a mental shift in the way we think about things.

When Somerset County, England, changed their traffic system from lights to no lights, the townsfolk thought it wouldn't work. "Drivers are not going to dovetail in," they said. Surprisingly (to most citizens), after the traffic lights were removed, the queues instantly disappeared. It was less congested and easier for pedestrians to cross the street. A drive through town that used to take twenty minutes now took just five minutes. The difference was extraordinary.

It took some time for people to adjust. Most people were used to just looking at the lights. Some drivers still assumed the right of way in the time-honored fashion dictated by traffic controls. Reform required a change in culture, and people had to unlearn their bad habits. It was a new way of thinking that required a mind shift, and it took a while for people to catch on, but it resulted in a system that was ultimately safer and faster.

The same is true when moving to a Lean kanban flow approach. It's new and different. People think it won't work, and there is resistance across teams and departments. Culture change is often required to unlearn bad habits. The results are rarely as instantaneous as the traffic light example, but often people see some improvement early on in the form of fewer interruptions, more transparency, and a faster flow of work.

Theory and expertise in the science of quantitative measures is a valuable part of exposing time thievery and improving workflow. It interests me, and so I've dabbled in it. It's the math—I like solving for x. My first ambition was to be a detective like Honey West. I've experienced firsthand the power to influence decisions using metrics. I've gotten budget and headcount approvals and agreement to pursue one direction over another because of metrics. I've applied them in the interest of improving the world of work.

But theory and metrics is not why I do this work. Articulating abstract or unintuitive ideas *viva voce* is not my strong suit. My brain competes with my own narrative. The reason I know a lot about making work visible is because in many ways (maybe in most ways), it's easier for me to communicate visually than vocally. The act of making work and ideas visible so that people can easily see the problem or situation is exciting. Creating useful, relevant, visually available and beautiful information to help people understand what's really going on is a true delight. But it's not why I do this work.

I do this work because I get to connect with people at an intrinsic level. I can sense what people are dealing with from watching them at work and during workshops. Much of it comes from instinct while observing people. Ideas just come to me for how to visually shine a light on their pain. I see what's happening at the emotional level and transform it into a physical visual to help people communicate. For me, interpreting other people's energy to understand their situation is an automatic process. I'm a visual empathic listener, and this is what I do best. Put me in the crime scene and let me deduce away.

I would not be able to do this work without the ability to make work visible, optimize for flow, and enable important discussions. I've provided you with some of the essential tools and knowledge necessary to do the things that will help you become the voice of reason in your organization. It's now up to you to take these tools and run with them.

Stop banging your head against a system that doesn't work. The practices in this book can put you in a position to continuously experience improvements. Small improvements over time make a difference. So get out there and encourage others to join you in your journey to do the right thing. I hope I have inspired you to get started. Just start doing the exercises, visualizing the problems, and provoking the necessary conversations, and see where these actions lead you.

I doubt that I've covered everything you need to know to successfully expose your time thieves and optimize your workflow, but I've tried my best, which is all any of us can do. There are many aspects of visualizing and improving workflow that I am still learning.

When I first thought about writing this book, my brain seemed to be overflowing with ideas and examples for how everyday workers trapped in corporate bureaucracy or business stalemate could improve their world and could become the voice of reason in their organization. And that's who I wanted to reach/teach—the everyday person just trying to do a good job and enable their team to reach a better place. A happier place. So, carry on. If I can do it, so can you.

Good luck!

GLOSSARY

A3: Named after the international paper size of 11 x 17 inch (297 x 420 mm) piece of paper, an A3 is used to structure discussions to gain understanding and agreement.

AGILE: Incremental and iterative improvements done on a regular cadence; an alternative to traditional project management methods, suggests frequent reassessment and adaptation of plans.

BOOLEAN LOGIC: A form of algebra in which all values are either *true* or *false* and represented in the binary numbering system where each digit has a value of either 1 or 0.

BUILD: When code is collected from a source code repository, compiled into executables, and packaged up with all the necessary parts to be installed into a place where the resulting new functionality is seen by others.

CAPACITY UTILIZATION: The percentage of the total possible capacity that is used. If a person has the capacity to work 10 hours a day and they work 7 hours, then their capacity utilization is 70%.

CHURN: Customers or subscribers who cut ties with your service or company.

CONSTRAINT: A bottleneck in the system; something preventing forward movement.

CONTEXT SWITCH: The act of stopping work on one thing to start work on a different thing, due to an interruption.

COST OF DELAY (COD): A way of communicating value and urgency, CoD is a measure of the impact of time on valuable outcomes.

COUNTERMEASURES: Actions taken to counteract a problem.

CYCLE TIME: The elapsed time it takes to complete a request from the time the work began to the time the work was delivered.

DEPENDENCY: Files required in order for source code to compile; people with specialized skill-sets needed to do something; an event that needs to occur before something else can be achieved.

DEPLOYMENT LEAD TIME: The elapsed time it takes to build and deploy a change once code is checked in to source control.

ECONOMIES OF SCALE: A concept in economics that relates a decrease in cost with an increase in production; the cost advantage that arises with increased output of a product.

ENTERPRISE RESOURCE PLANNING (ERP) SYSTEM: A management information system that integrates elements such as planning, purchasing, inventory, sales, marketing, finance, and HR.

ENVIRONMENT ISSUES: Problems with the configuration of servers that prevent websites and other things from working correctly.

FAILURE DEMAND: Demand caused by a failure to do something or to do something right for the customer.

FEATURE DRIVEN DEVELOPMENT: A type of Agile development focused on cross-functional, collaborative, and time-boxed activities to build features.

FIRST-IN, FIRST-OUT (FIFO): A prioritization method where work is processed in a first-in, first-out fashion.

FLOW: Value pulled through a system smoothly and predictably; the positive aspects and joy of being "in the zone."

FLOW EFFICIENCY: The percentage of time where work is done vs. waiting for work to be done. Calculate it by dividing work time by work + wait time.

GANTT CHART: The illustration of the start and finish dates of all steps in a project.

KANBAN: Japanese word for visual signal; used throughout this book to refer to a visual management pull system for knowledge work.

KINGMAN'S FORMULA: Used to calculate a utilization percentage from the relationship between WIP and flow times. It shows how wait times increase dramatically as utilization approaches 100%.

LEAD TIME: A measure of the elapsed time it takes to work on a request from when it was first requested to when it was delivered to the customer.

LEAN: A Socratic philosophy used to make improvements. Lean puts just-in-time practices and visual management front and center.

PULL SYSTEM: When new work is pulled into the system based on available capacity to handle it; where the people doing the work have autonomy to start it when they have time.

QUEUE: A pileup of work waiting on attention to be worked on; work that is in a wait state.

RESOURCE EFFICIENCY: The percentage of time that resources are busy. Sometimes referred to as keeping people busy all the time.

SCRUM: An Agile framework used to complete projects.

SILVER BULLET: An urgent request to do something right away; usually, initiated by someone in a leadership position.

SMOKE TEST: A test to ensure that code functions as expected after a build is completed.

SOURCE CONTROL: A place where developers check in their code for safe keeping.

STAND-UP: A brief (usually 15 minutes) meeting where a team discusses issues. Because it's only 15 minutes, people stand up for it.

SUNK COST FALLACY: When you keep doing something because you've put a lot of effort into it and you don't want to waste that effort.

SYSTEM: A network of interdependent components that work together to try to accomplish a goal; includes the people doing the work and the impacting rules and tools.

SYSTEMS THINKING: A holistic view of the system where the goal is to optimize the whole system versus just individual functions or silos.

TECHNICAL DEBT: Extra effort required to fix software bugs and develop new features because of previous quick and dirty design choices.

THEORY OF CONSTRAINTS (TOC): A way to identify the most important limiting factor (the constraint) that stands in the way of achieving a goal and then system-atically improving that constraint until it is no longer the limiting factor.

THROUGHPUT: The number of things completed over a period of time.

TIME-BOX: A specific period of time with a distinct start and end time. Ex: Pencils down after the two hour exam that began precisely at noon.

VALUE STREAM: The activities done from beginning to end for a specific product or service in order to provide business value.

VELOCITY: The number of story points completed over a period of time (usually two weeks).

WATERFALL APPROACH: A traditional software development method where work cannot proceed until all the parts of the entire previous stage complete.

WEIGHTED SHORTEST JOB FIRST (SWJF): A prioritization method where the job that has the shortest duration is processed before other jobs of equal value.

WORKFLOW: The flow of work through the pipeline (or system) from beginning to end.

WORK-IN-PROGRESS (WIP): All the work started but not yet finished.

WORK ITEM: Anything being worked on; work that encompasses effort both large and small.

WORK STATE: The state that the work is in. Work flows through different states on its way to completion. The work states show us where the work is in the pipeline.

ENDNOTES

INTRODUCTION

1. *In Time*, directed by Andrew Niccol (Los Angeles: 20th Century Fox, 2011), DVD.

2. Darren Davis, "The Secret History of Kanban by Darren Davis [Guest Post]," *Northwest Cadence*, February 19, 2015, http://blog.nwcadence.com/the-secret-history-of-kanban-by-darren-davis/.

3. Kate Murphy, "No Time to Think," *The New York Times*, July 25, 2014, http://www.nytimes.com/2014/07/27/sunday-review/no-time-to-think.html.

4. Niklas Modig and Pär Åhlström, *This is Lean: Resolving the Efficiency Paradox*, (Stockholm: Rheologica Publishing, 2016), Introduction.

5. W. Edwards Deming, as quoted in John Hunter, "A Bad System Will Beat a Good Person Every Time," *The W. Edwards Deming Institute Blog*, February 26, 2015, https://blog.deming.org/2015/02/a-bad-system-will-beat-a-good-person-every-time/.

PART 1

1.1 1. Vanessa Bohns, "Why Is It So Hard to Say No?," interview by Jeremy Hobson, *Here and Now*, March 31, 2014, www.wbur.org/hereand now/2014/03/31/saying-no-psychology.

2. Todd Watts, "Addressing the Detrimental Effects of Context Switching with DevOps," *DevOps Blog*, Software Engineering Institute at Carnegie Mellon University, March 5, 2015, https://insights.sei.cmu.edu/devops/2015/03/addressing-the-detrimental-effects-of-context-switching-with-devops.html.

3. "Context Switching," OSDev.org, last modified December 29, 2015, http://wiki.osdev.org/Context_Switching.

4. Harry F. Harlow, as quoted in Daniel H. Pink, *Drive: The Surprising Truth about What Motivates Us*, (New York: Riverhead Books, 2011), 3.

5. "The Hounds of Baskerville," *Sherlock*, directed by Paul McGuigan, written by Mark Gatiss, aired on January 8, 2012, on BBC.

6. David Rock, *Your Brain at Work: Strategies for Overcoming Distraction, Regaining Focus, and Working Smarter All Day Long*, (New York: Harper Business, 2009), 47.

7. Edward R. Tufte, *Envisioning Information*, (Cheshire, CT: Graphics Press, 2013), 50.

8. Dan Weatbrook, personal conversation with author, 2015.

1.2 1. Troy Magennis, "Entangled: Solving the Hairy Problem of Team Dependencies," Agile Alliance conference video, 1:15:15, August 5, 2015, https://www.agilealliance.org/resources/videos/entangled-solving-the-hairy -problem-of-team-dependencies/.

2. Maura Thomas, "Your Team's Time Management Problem Might Be a Focus Problem," *Harvard Business Review*, February 28, 2017, https://hbr.org /2017/02/your-teams-time-management-problem-might-be-a-focus-problem.

1.3 1. *2016 State of DevOps Report*, (Portland, OR: Puppet Labs, 2016) 26, https://puppet.com/resources/whitepaper/2016-state-of-devops-report.

1.4 1. Ross Garber, as quoted in Gary Keller, *The ONE Thing: The Surprisingly Simple Truth Behind Extraordinary Results* (London: John Murray, 2013), 19.

1.5 1. Michael Feathers, *Working Effectively with Legacy Code*, (Upper Saddle River, NJ: Prentice Hall, 2004), xvi.

2. Donald G. Reinertsen, *The Principles of Product Development Flow: Second Generation Lean Product Development* (Redondo Beach: Celeritas, 2009), 152.

3. Reinertsen, *The Principles of Product Development Flow*, 47.

PART II

1. Colin Ware, *Information Visualization: Perception for Design*, (San Francisco: Morgan Kaufman, 2000), 2.

2. Ware, Information Visualization, 2.

3. Linda Kreger Silverman, *Upside-Down Brilliance: The Visual-Spatial Learner.* (Denver: DeLeon Gifted Development Center, 1999), www.gifteddevelopment.com.

2.1   1.   Philippe Kruchten, *What Colour is Your Backlog*, presentation, July 7, 2011, https://pkruchten.files.wordpress.com/2012/07/kruchten-110707-what-colours-is-your-backlog-2up.pdf.

2.   Silverman, *Upside-Down Brilliance.*

2.3   1.   Cornelia Davis, personal conversation with author, April 2017.

2.4   1.   Wikipedia, "Pomodoro Technique," last modified April 10, 2017, https://en.wikipedia.org/wiki/Pomodoro_Technique.

2.   Langdon Morris, *High Performance Organizations in a Wicked Problem World* (Walnut Creek, CA: Innovation Labs, 2004), http://www.innovationlabs.com/high_performance.pdf.

2.5   1.   Daniel Kahneman, *Thinking Fast and Slow* (New York. Farrar, Straus and Giroux, 2015), 4.

2.   "Cost of Delay," *BlackSwanFarming.com*, accessed April 22, 2017, http://blackswanfarming.com/cost-of-delay/.

2.7   1.   Julia Wester, "Visualizing More than Just Work with Kanban Boards," *EverydayKanban.com*, March 9, 2016, http://www.everydaykanban.com/2016/03/09/visualizing-more-than-just-work-with-kanban-boards/#housemove.

2.   Jim Benson and Tonianne DeMaria Barry, *Personal Kanban: Mapping Work, Navigating Life* (Seattle, WA: Modus Cooperandi Press, 2011), 158–159.

PART III

3.1 1. Wikipedia, "Hofstadter's law," last modified February 12, 2017,
            https://en.wikipedia.org/wiki/Hofstadter%27s_law.

2. Daniel S. Vacanti, *Actionable Agile Metrics for Predictability: An Introduction*
    (Victoria, BC: Leanpub, 2015), 51–53.

3. Reinertsen, *The Principles of Product Development* Flow, 59.

4. Kaomi Goetz, "How 3M Gave Everyone Days Off and Created an Innovation
    Dynamo," Co.Design, February 1, 2011.

5. Goetz, "How 3M Gave Everyone Days Off."

3.4 1. "Lean Coffee Lives Here," Lean Coffee, accessed May 29, 2017,
            http://leancoffee.org/

2. Adam Yuret, *How to Have Great Meetings: A Lean Coffee Book* (Seattle, WA:
    Context Driven Agility Press, 2016).

3.5 1. David McCandless, "What Makes a Good Data Visualization,"
            InformationIsBeautiful.net, accessed July 2017,
            http://www.informationisbeautiful.net/2015/what-makes-a-good-
            data-visualization.

CONCLUSION

1. Jared M. Spool, "The Quiet Death of the Major Re-Launch," UIE, August 7, 2006,
    https://articles.uie.com/death_of_relaunch/.

2. Klaus Leopold and Siegfried Kaltenecker, *Kanban Change Leadership: Creating
    a Culture of Continuous Improvement*, (Hoboken, NJ: Wiley, 2015), 277.

ACKNOWLEDGMENTS

I could not have written *Making Work Visible* without the support of Todd Sattersten. Todd believed in the allure of this book when I wasn't so sure. He laid the foundation and put the wheels in motion to make it all possible. Todd has keen instincts and a knack for attending to the most crucial aspects of book publishing.

It has been my extreme pleasure to work with the remarkable Anna Noak. Anna has got to be the most supportive and dedicated editorial director in the business. She coached me through the entire writing and publishing process during weekends, holidays, and vacations with the spirit of an astute master. As a novice illustrator, I was extremely lucky to have designer Joy Stauber's guidance on color and image design. I also appreciate how generous Sylvia Cottrell, Sarah Heilman, and Leah Brown were with their editorial talents.

Writing *Making Work Visible* has been a way for me to consolidate and reflect on the things I've learned while teaching and coaching teams on Lean, kanban, and flow—any colleagues and friends have influenced me over the course of my career while learning my trade whom I'd like to thank, especially the team at Corbis for all the collaboration during the early experimental years: Larry Cohen, Darren Davis, Sandy Thompson, Eli Hurst, Jay Freer, Calvin Nguyen, Dwayne Johnson, Debbie Earle, Suzanne Bagdon, Jason Birklid, and Rick Garber.

I had numerous teachers who helped me to learn Agile and Lean practices whom I want to thank, including David J. Anderson, Daniel Vacanti, Chris Hefley, Ian Carroll, Mattias Jansson, Arne

Roock, Liz Keogh, Torbjörn Gyllebring, Mattias Skarin, Yuval Yuret, Karl Scotland, David Joyce, Katherine Kirk, Klaus Leopold, Markus Andrezak, Pawel Brodzinski, Hakan Forss, Joakim Sundén, Eric Willeke, Don Reinertsen, Mike Burrows, Jim Benson, Russell Healy, Steve Holt, Michael Cheveldave, Jeff Anderson, Jason Yip, Jon Terry, Gaetano Mazzanti, and Joshua Arnold.

Troy Magennis, whose work on dependencies I profile in sections 1.2 and 2.3, has become an extraordinary mentor and friend. I met Troy at Corbis where we shared an office together and where I experienced first hand his influential writing and coaching. It was in that office where I first dreamed that maybe one day, I too might write a book. I am proud to be one of his many devotees and friends.

At DevOpsDays Seattle 2016, Pauly Comtois unveiled one of his first hand-drawn presentations which inspired me to do the same. Later that year, David O'Neal shared his talented drawing technique with me. Many thanks to them both—my presentations have never been the same since.

I am especially grateful for the kindness, encouragement, and inclusiveness during my first interactions with the DevOps community, who inspired me in 2011/2012, and still do to this day, to practice my learnings: Patrick Debois, John Vincent, Damon Edwards, Andrew Clay Shafer, Stephen Nelson-Smith, John Willis, Jez Humble, Ben Rockwood, Mandi Walls, Jennifer Davis, Tom Sulston, Michael Rembetsy, Marius Ducea, Adrian Cockcroft, Karthik Gaekwad, James Wickett, Ernest Mueller, and Sascha Bates.

It has been my absolute pleasure to work with the talented Chris Hefley and Julia Wester. Their tremendous support and feedback, during the early draft of the book, and this book benefited tremendously from their review and input.

The articulate feedback and enthusiasm I received from the one and only Gene Kim kept me in check and helped me persevere to the end.

I owe a special debt to Torianne DeMaria who penned the foreword for me while on vacation sailing. Her writing brings me pure joy with the magnificent words and expertise she sheds on us all to learn.

And to my beloved husband, Joseph, who is the most generous person on earth. During the writing of this book, he took over household and garden duties on many a weekend and holiday so I could write. He made me tea, made me food, and made me smile.

ddegrandis.com
Learnings on flow

@dominicad

A NOTE ON THE TYPE

The text of *Making Work Visible* was set in Chaparral Pro and DIN 2014.

Chaparral Pro was created by the legendary and award winning type designer Carol Twombly. Released in 1997, Chaparral was Twombly's last typeface before retiring. It combines the legibility of slab serif designs popularized in the 19th century with the grace of 16th-century roman book lettering. A part of the Adobe Originals family of typefaces, Chaparral has varying letter proportions with thick and thin strokes, creating a friendly appearance and was used in the body text to give a lovely visual finish to the illustrations throughout the book.

DIN 2014 is a contemporary version of the well-known DIN typeface. DIN stands for Deutsches Institut für Normung (German Institute for Standardization.) The DIN 1451 typeface was designed in 1936 for road and railway signage. The typeface was designed by Vasily Biryukov and released by Paratype in 2015. The Regular is most often used in long text settings, while Light and Bold faces are extremely well proportioned at large sizes, which can be seen in the striking part, chapter, and section headers in the pages of this book.

...

Printed and bound by Worzalla, Stevens Point, Wisconsin